Contents

Appendixes

Bibliography   *153*

Index   *155*

Chapter 1 The Value of a Tutoring Program

Successful reading depends on building habits of mind.

Reading is not a straightforward activity. In recent years, we have discovered just how complex a task it really is; the International Reading Association confirms that before readers can construct meaning from the symbols in front of them, their brains have to integrate many different mental processes (*On Reading,* 2004).

For many of us, though, reading is an everyday activity, and like breathing, we easily take it for granted. We may get caught up in an author's explanation of something that fascinates us or lost in a favorite story, rarely stopping to think about how we translate markings upon a page into mental images. It is as if by magic that understanding happens.

Not all of us are that fortunate. For a significant number of people, reading remains a difficult and daunting task, one that places severe limitations on their lives. Across Canada and the United States, reports since 2004 conclude that, depending on jurisdiction and social and cultural factors, anywhere from 25 to 50 percent of students are at risk of not graduating from high school (Green and Winters 2006). In North America, boys are more profoundly affected, with the gender gap significantly larger for students of racial minorities. The single most important factor associated with this risk is the lack of literacy skills.

The ramifications for students without adequate literacy skills are lifelong and profound. With the advent of the technological and information global society, the gap between the literate and those whose literacy skills are weak is widening more and more—to the detriment of individuals and societies alike (Murray 2006).

A Program Based on Effective Reading Instruction

The disparity between competent and struggling readers raises important questions. Why is it that an activity that comes so easily to many people remains challenging for others? Why is it that something which provides so much pleasure and enjoyment for one group of people remains a source of constant frustration and aggravation for another? What role might tutoring play to redress the balance? And how can we use tutoring to help individuals in the latter group become members of the first?

Competent readers integrate the different mental processes involved with reading subconsciously—struggling readers may be unaware of

Organizations Involved in Literacy Development
International Reading Association (IRA): www.reading.org

National Council of Teachers of English: www.ncte.org

Australian Association of Teachers of English: www.aate.org.au

them. A reading tutor, supported by the classroom teacher, can help make these processes conscious and reinforce them for struggling readers.

In this book, we present a tutoring program based on the principles of effective reading instruction. These principles derive from what professional teaching organizations have found true in literacy development.

The International Reading Association, the National Council of Teachers of English, and the Australian Association of Teachers of English all call for reading instruction that

- approaches each person as an individual with valued and distinct language, experience, and culture that provide the basis for further language development
- nurtures both self-esteem and competence in reading
- provides a variety of reading approaches and strategies to support learners in constructing meaning from text
- develops language and critical thinking skills through explicit instruction related to vocabulary, fluency, and comprehension
- grows out of close observation and documentation of learners' strengths, interests, and reading needs
- provides texts and experiences that extend learners' understandings of language, themselves, and the world around them
- teaches learners how to control and improve their own literacy

The approaches of the tutoring program outlined here build on these principles of effective reading instruction.

In particular, this tutoring program emphasizes that tutors should build strong relationships with the students they tutor, valuing them as individuals and developing trust. We encourage tutors to catch up on the lives of their students at the start of each tutoring session—too often, this time is the only one-to-one personal time with an older individual that many students receive. This powerful kind of support is critical to all youth, but especially to those struggling with reading.

This program then calls upon tutors to build on information from the classroom teacher and the continual new knowledge they gain of their students. Tutors apply this knowledge to plan and implement tutoring experiences that work from student strengths and interests, addressing specific reading goals through explicit instruction. To the greatest extent possible, tutors and students should collaborate in goal setting, monitoring of reading growth, and choice of reading activities: giving students as much voice as possible supports their path to independent reading. These approaches have particular importance for students reading below grade-level expectations.

The Need to Teach Cueing Systems

Some people refer to the mental processes that interact during reading as *processing systems*; others refer to them as *cueing systems*. (See *Beginning to Read: Thinking and Learning about Print* by Marilyn Adams and *Guiding the Reading Process* by David Booth.) However they are viewed, research has shown that skilled readers use these systems subconsciously.

Usually, people who read poorly must be taught these systems explicitly and then shown how to use them consciously until they are internalized. Even highly skilled independent readers return to conscious use of these systems when a text does not make sense to them: they reread a passage, consciously attending to specific words and word meanings, working to make meaning until their interpretation makes sense.

Cueing systems generally refer to the following aspects of written language:

- **Orthographic cues:** knowledge about letters, letter patterns, and systems of spelling. (From the Greek words *ortho*, for straight, and *graph*, for write)
- **Phonographemic cues:** knowledge about the sounds of letters and letter combinations; also referred to as *phonics cues*. (From the Greek words *phono*, for voice, and *graph*, for write)
- **Syntactic cues:** knowledge about language, including larger language patterns of sentences and word functions of nouns, verbs, adjectives, and so on. This knowledge, for instance, includes the reader's awareness that a sentence must contain a verb. (From the Greek words *syn*, for together, and *tassein*, for arrange)
- **Semantic cues:** knowledge about the meaning of words and of the culture of the topic. In order to understand how words are being used in a given passage, the reader must understand the world of the topic. For instance, the terms *motion, work,* and *energy* carry different meanings and connotations in physics than they do in daily life. (From the Greek word *semainen,* to signify)
- **Pragmatic cues:** knowledge about the appearance of text on a page; this includes knowledge about the differences in how we read a poem versus a prose text; about the use of headings and subheads; and about the use of bullets and font features, such as size, bolding, and italicizing.

These terms are essential for tutors to know. With other key terms, they are summarized on a reproducible resource, "Terms for Tutors," at the end of this chapter. The various kinds of cues help readers predict what they are going to read, both in terms of the larger construction of meaning and also in terms of anticipating specific words and phrases that they expect to find in the text.

In tutoring situations, effective tutors help dependent readers learn to activate these systems before they read. First, students become aware of the systems; then, they come to ask themselves what alerts them to the kind of meaning they can expect to find. Next, they learn to use these systems fluidly, and finally, they learn to activate the systems as *habits of mind* every time they get ready to read. Students need to understand that these habits of mind ensure success for independent readers.

First, though, classroom teachers need to introduce tutors to a conscious understanding of these systems in the initial training session. Also through periodic meetings with tutors, teachers reinforce articulation and use of these systems in the tutoring sessions. Over time, tutors who volunteer year after year come to implement these processes as a natural part of the tutoring process.

Habits of Mind
By using the term *habits of mind*, we are emphasizing how mental processes are automatically activated every time a skilled reader picks up a text. Continual use of these processes is key to independent reading. Skilled readers use these processes subconsciously; however, less skilled readers require explicit instruction and continual reinforcement for their use to become habitual. Teachers will initially need to explain and model these processes for tutors and then reinforce their use, particularly in the first month of tutoring.

The Potential of One-to-One Teaching

One-to-one teaching is recognized as the most effective strategy for helping learners with reading challenges (Clay 1993; Wasik and Slavin 1993). Of course, it is not possible for teachers to work with all of their students one-to-one. A powerful way to achieve the benefits of one-to-one teaching and learning is to use trained volunteer tutors.

Not only is one-to-one tutoring highly effective in helping students become independent readers, it is also extremely satisfying for tutors and learners alike. Tutors are in a unique position to build trusting relationships with their assigned students. Students come to rely on their tutors, confide in them, and see them as people they can trust. In turn, tutors can become mentors who model good reading practices to their students. By expressing out loud what they do subconsciously as they read, they increase their students' awareness of the habits of fluent readers and demonstrate what the students themselves must do to become successful readers.

The International Reading Association (2000) states, "No single method or single combination of methods can successfully teach children to read." The IRA position reinforces the fact that people learn to read in a variety of ways. No one method works for everyone. The best approach is to use a combination of approaches, tailoring instruction to the learner's needs and what works for the learner. The tutoring model we propose does precisely that. It ensures that explicit attention is given to the different cueing systems in a program that balances reading and writing activities through the use of authentic text that interests the learner.

Given that reading requires the interaction of many processes, a tutor might feel overwhelmed about where to begin. Support of the classroom teacher is critical for the novice tutor. As tutors gain more experience, the degree of support they need decreases dramatically, and conversations between teachers and tutors who have worked with the teachers for several years become much more reciprocal. Novice tutors, though, need support in learning how to become good reading tutors.

Typically, novice tutors bring enthusiasm, a deep belief in the importance of reading, and a commitment to others. It is precisely these characteristics that can make them somewhat anxious in the early stages of tutoring. Classroom teachers have an important role to play in these early stages. They need to support tutors by providing a training session and giving tutors texts that will probably appeal to their particular students and be at the appropriate reading level. Consistent communication with tutors about the specifics of tutoring is essential, as are periodic meetings. Increasingly, tutors will be able to supply texts of interest to their students, but the classroom teacher needs to supply content-area texts if they are being used, with directions to the tutor. The teacher also needs to remain alert to possible texts of interest that the tutor might use.

In one-to-one tutoring, tutors guided by teachers can work with their students in selecting the texts to be read and the approaches to be used. They can build from the students' specific strengths and interests to address their individual needs. By using a variety of strategies and explicit teaching, tutors help learners build *habits of mind* for successful

The presence of "Terms for Tutors" on the next pages recognizes that tutors require training and that much of their work is based on making visible to their students what comes to them automatically and subconsciously.

reading and a repertoire of reading strategies that they will be able to draw upon.

Even the least skilled and least experienced tutors can offer what dependent readers need most. Our research shows that the strongest contribution that tutors can make to the success of the people they are tutoring is to value them as individuals and believe that they can improve their reading. Tutor persistence and commitment help motivate learners and strengthen their belief in themselves.

Tutoring is about support in the ongoing process of improving reading. The small steps and gains that occur boost learners' confidence and give them the incentive to keep on working. For older students, this affective, or emotional, support often comes at a time when they have lost much faith in themselves. The tutors' gift to them is a literacy ticket which will help them become active participants in the world.

Terms for Tutors

Independent readers use cueing systems fluidly, moving between the various systems subconsciously to predict what they are going to read about. They also make conscious use of the systems when a text is not making sense to them: they reread a passage, attending to specific words and word meanings, working on meaning making until their interpretation makes sense.

Dependent readers usually need to be taught these systems explicitly and shown how to use them consciously. In tutoring situations, the goal is to help readers learn to activate these systems as a *habit of mind* every time they get ready to read. Enabling readers to develop this habit of mind ensures their success. Tutors aid dependent readers in recognizing and internalizing these types of cues:

Cueing Systems

Orthographic cues: knowledge about letters, letter patterns, and systems of spelling.

Phonographemic cues: knowledge about the sounds of letters and letter combinations; also referred to as *phonics cues*.

Syntactic cues: knowledge about language including larger language patterns of sentences and the word functions of nouns, verbs, adjectives, and so on. This knowledge, for instance, includes the reader's awareness that a sentence must contain a verb.

Semantic cues: knowledge about the meaning of words and of the culture of the topic. For instance, the terms *motion*, *work* and *energy* carry different meanings and connotations in physics than they do in daily life. In order to understand how words are being used in a given passage, the reader must understand the world of the topic.

Pragmatic cues: knowledge about the appearance of text on a page, for example, about the differences in how to read a poem versus a prose text; about the use of headings and subheads; and about the use of bullets and font features such as size, bolding, italicizing.

Terms Related to Word Recognition

Knowing some basic definitions will help tutors teach word recognition strategies. These definitions will enable them to become aware of techniques that independent readers have internalized.

First of all, words consist of rimes and onsets. A **rime** is a vowel and any consonants that follow it in a syllable. In *hit*, *-it* is the rime and in *drool*, *-ool* is the rime. Sometimes, these are called *word families*. Examples include *hit*, *bit*, and *sit* or *drool*, *pool*, and *fool*. An **onset** is the consonant prior to the vowel. In *hit*, *h* is the onset and in *drool*, *dr* is the onset.

Phonemes are the smallest units of sound in a language that are represented by letters or combinations of letters. For example, the word "little" has four phonemes: /l/, /i/, /t/, /l/.
The diagonal marks indicate the *sounds* rather than the letters.

Graphemes are the graphic representations of sounds. In western languages, these are the letters or letter combinations that represent sounds. For example, the word "little" has six letters, but only four sounds [*litl*]. Note that the same word may have a different number of graphemes and phonemes.

Morphemes are the smallest meaningful parts of words. These include prefixes, suffixes, and root words: they are the building blocks for more complex words. A **prefix** is an element placed at the beginning of a word to adjust or qualify its meaning; a **suffix** is an element added at the end of a word to form a derivative. Either or both elements are attached to a **root word** to modify its meaning.

Terms for Tutors (continued)

Sample prefixes are *un-*, *re-*, and *im-*. Sample suffixes are *-ed*, *-ing*, and *-est*. A sample root word is *read*, from which words such as *reread*, *reader*, and *reading* can be created.

Some Common Morphemes

Prefixes

bi-, di-	two (*bicycle*, *divide*)
con-, com-	with, together (*conversation*)
dis-	away, not (*disagree*)
mis-	bad, badly (*misinform*)
non-	not (*nonsense*)
pre-	before (*predict*)
re-	again; back (*reread*)
sub-	under; below (*submarine*)
tri-	three (*tripod*)
un-	not (*unhappy*)

Suffixes

-er	more; person who does something (*bigger*, *painter*)
-est	most (*biggest*)
-ful	having a particular quality; full of (*hopeful*)
-ish	like something; having a particular quality (*foolish*)
-ist	person who studies or practises something (*artist*)
-less	without (*careless*, *homeless*)
-ly	in a certain way; changes an adjective into an adverb (*sadly*, *quickly*)
-ness	state of being; changes an adjective, or descriptive word, into a noun (*happiness*)
-tion	changes a verb into a noun (*connection*, *formation*)

Chapter 2 Setting Up a Volunteer Tutoring Program

Successful tutoring programs do not just happen: they require clear expectations, monitoring, and support. As well, they must be realistic. The classroom teacher, the student being tutored, and the tutor will likely devote additional personal time to the endeavor.

Everyone needs to be aware of the extra time that others give both in terms of fulfilling their own responsibilities and in setting their expectations of others. In this program, we expect tutors to prepare for each tutoring session by writing a brief plan, by looking for texts likely to interest their students, and by providing necessary materials, such as file cards with words that their students will be learning. Similarly, we expect the classroom teacher to ensure that tutors are trained, to identify passages in any content-area texts that may be used during tutoring, and to note specific content areas that tutors should emphasize. Teacher monitoring and support of the tutor is important throughout any tutoring program.

Over more than ten years, we have built the research-based model of tutoring reported in this book, and we continue to conduct research on its effectiveness. We know that it is important for tutors to prepare for tutoring sessions, choosing from a prescribed set of activities to address specific learner needs. We also know of the importance of building a relationship early and of making time in each tutoring session to deepen that relationship.

In this chapter, we discuss how to set up a successful tutoring program. We look at the active recruitment of volunteers, roles, responsibilities, training, and realistic expectations.

Define the Role and Responsibilities of Tutors

Before tutors can even be found, their role must be defined so that potential volunteers have a clear understanding of how much time will be expected, exactly when and where they will conduct the tutoring, and how long the tutoring will be. Clear expectations will help ensure that tutors are consistent in their attendance, a critical factor for successful tutoring and for building the habits of mind necessary for independent reading. We recommend offering "Expectations for Tutors" to prospective volunteers.

Expectations for Tutors

Welcome to our school's tutoring program!

We are grateful to you for offering your time to work with our students. The one-to-one attention students receive through the tutoring program is often critical not only to students' skill development, but also to their sense of themselves.

The relationship that tutors and students build is the foundation of successful tutoring. It is so rewarding to tutors and students alike, providing students with motivation to tackle what is hard work for them and providing deep satisfaction to tutors. Through the consistent presence and non-judgmental acceptance of their tutors, students feel valued and worthy. This feeling is a gift from their tutors—one that often changes their lives.

Although the tutoring itself is one-to-one, the tutoring program involves classroom teachers and parents/guardians as partners, as well. We have found that setting the following expectations of tutors ensures a successful program.

- Get a police screening check and take that to the first meeting with the classroom teacher.
- Attend a training session to be held by the classroom teacher or school tutor coordinator at a mutually convenient time.
- Plan to tutor twice weekly for about 45 minutes, including time to catch up on what your assigned students have been doing.
- Tutor for a minimum of ten weeks.
- From the classroom teacher, get initial information about the strengths, interests, and needs of each of the students being tutored. Then, add to this list as you learn more about your students over the course of the tutoring program. Be sure to share the new information with the teacher.
- Throughout the tutoring, plan periodic meetings with the classroom teacher to discuss specifics of tutoring goals and progress.
- For every tutoring session, arrive at the school early enough or stay after the session to communicate with the classroom teacher—have tutoring plans and resources ready. Be as flexible as possible when it comes to finding mutually convenient times to meet. As you can appreciate, classroom teachers have many responsibilities.
- Establish and maintain positive rapport with each student being tutored.
- Conduct informal diagnostic reading appraisals of learners at the beginning of the tutoring program and again at the end.
- Complete mid-tutoring and end-of-tutoring reports for school use and for parents/guardians, showing initial drafts to the classroom teacher and revising the letters based on suggestions received.
- Maintain a tutoring binder, with tutoring plans, reflections, and resources.
- Maintain a *literacy portfolio*, that is, a collection of student work completed during tutoring sessions. This portfolio can be part of the tutoring binder.
- Show initiative in finding or creating specific strategic tutoring materials, for example:
  - texts that appeal to learner interests and are at an appropriate reading level (Check with the classroom teacher, special education teacher, or librarian for assistance when needed.)
  - materials that the learner can manipulate, such as flash cards or word games, to reinforce word recognition and comprehension activities
  - materials that support kinesthetic learning, such as texts for Readers Theatre or a small ball for the student to squeeze while reading (Resource teachers for students through Grade 8 may well have materials that are relevant; in a secondary school, check the personal learning centre for materials.)
  - school computer software applications that might be used, such as *Kidspiration, Inspiration* or *Smart Ideas*
  - appropriate Internet sites and magazine resources

Recruit Volunteer Tutors

Once you have established expectations for volunteers, you are ready to seek them out. Our experience is that people who volunteer to be reading tutors are usually very well suited for the task. Nevertheless, it is important to ensure that some kind of initial screening is in place. Unless the school has a prior relationship with a post-secondary institution where tutors are assigned school placements, all tutors should be interviewed, even briefly, by the school and asked to submit the names of up to three people who can be called for a telephone reference check—in reference checks, one is looking for reliability, trustworthiness in working with youth, judgment, commitment, and available time. We do *not* look for prior knowledge of reading or tutoring: that knowledge will come through experience with the tutoring program.

This reference check becomes the initial screening process for tutors. The training session held by the school provides a second screening process. Although not an explicit screen, the training session may help prospective tutors recognize that program expectations do not match their own, and they may choose not to continue. In our experience, only a few people withdraw. It is not worthwhile to try to convince people to remain if they feel that they cannot fully commit.

Initially, it may seem difficult to find tutors who wish to work with adolescents; there are, however, more potential volunteer tutors than might, at first, be apparent. It is surprising to discover just how many people are interested in working with students from ages 10 to 16. More males, for instance, prefer to work with young people in this age group than with younger children. It is just a matter of getting the program started and having the word spread of how rewarding it is to establish a relationship that is focused on something a student desperately needs in order to succeed in life.

Many elementary schools use older students as reading buddies: they provide good role models for their younger peers and listen to and encourage younger children. That is not the more sophisticated tutoring we are talking about here, though. The tutoring that we espouse requires training. Thus, a successful tutoring program requires older volunteers: people who can be trained and who can truly teach. Different types of volunteers make suitable tutors for adolescents. These include senior secondary school students, teacher education candidates, parents, retirees, and more. These are outlined more fully below.

Senior Secondary School Students

Some schools have courses where students in Grades 11 and 12 are taught about reading theory and complete tutoring placements, either with students in Grades 9 and 10 or in nearby junior high schools. The great advantage of this is that the tutors are being taught how to do the tutoring, a high school teacher meets with them frequently—usually two or three times weekly—and gives input and advice on the tutoring, and the tutors have accountability through the requirements of their own credit course. Tutors also have an opportunity to talk with other tutors and to share strategies and resources.

This source of tutors has a few disadvantages, though. Many high schools do not have such programs and it might take a couple of years to convince a school to mount such a program and to get it started. Another disadvantage is that, although the high school teacher provides continuity and tutor support, tutors remain for only one year. The school principal needs to be involved if teachers wish to establish a program in their own schools or in partnership with another school. The principal can more easily find out about the interest of other schools than can classroom teachers.

Teacher Education Candidates

Students enrolled in teacher education programs are a natural source of recruits for a tutoring program. Teacher candidates are looking for experience with young people, and some schools of education make tutoring a required part of their practicum experience.

Advantages are as above, except that the tutors bring more maturity, an established commitment to teaching, a stronger background in human development and learning, and strong initiative in the development of resources and activities. Depending on where they are in their own university programs, teacher education candidates may already have a strong background in these areas or it may still be developing.

A disadvantage to this group is that if teacher candidates are in one-year postgraduate programs, they will be available for one year only. In multi-year teacher education programs, though, teacher candidates often remain as tutors for more than one year, recognizing the value of the continued experience and of their connection to a single school. Teachers interested in having teacher candidates should contact the dean of the faculty or school of education.

Other University Students

In many universities, there are students who are not necessarily planning on going into teaching, but are interested in working with people. Increasingly, career centres in universities emphasize volunteer work as an important factor for successful job applications. Most universities have a volunteer placement office and a career centre: either is a good contact for volunteers.

Community College Students

Students in community college programs that prepare them for work as teacher assistants or for careers related to working with youth will also make well-informed and sensitive tutors. Like teacher candidates, they bring stronger backgrounds in pedagogy and in social aspects related to adolescent development than do many volunteers. Also like teacher candidates, these students may be available to tutor either for one year only or for two or three years, depending on their program of study.

Contact persons at a community college include the career centre or the dean or director of social service and education programs.

Community Volunteers, Including Retirees

North Americans are known for their volunteer capacity: community service is part of our ethic. A surprising number of people who are not fully employed make wonderful volunteer tutors. Community volunteers also have the potential to be involved for many years. Long-term involvement is the ideal, for the time spent both by the classroom teacher and the tutor in the first year pays dividends in successive years.

Similarly, many recently retired people are looking for something meaningful to do with their spare time. Reading experiences with their own children and grandchildren make them ideal tutors. Their work experience makes them acutely aware of the literacy requirements in the working world. Many retirees are eager to share their love of reading with young people.

When recruiting any volunteers, it is important that the school provide a single contact and establish a protocol for interviewing potential volunteers. Whether one teacher is looking for volunteers or several teachers are interested, the principal needs to be involved in establishing school protocols.

Recruiting from the wider community can be time consuming, but once the word gets out that the school is looking for volunteers and will train them, the number of volunteers will increase. A school can work through community volunteer centres. Beyond that, it can advertise with letter-size posters at places of worship, at recreational facilities, such as the local "Y," and in stores or centres that might attract the kind of volunteer the school wants to have—perhaps a bookstore or a seniors' centre.

Parents

Parents are often looking for ways to contribute to the school that their children attend. One way they can make a significant contribution is to serve as a reading tutor. It is recommended that they work in a classroom other than one attended by any of their own children. Contact with parents can be made in newsletters that are sent home and on the school's Web site.

Provide Tutor Training

Once tutors have been recruited, they need to be trained. We have found that the best way to end a training session is to let the tutors know whom they will be tutoring—it gives them a high. It is best for tutors to know in advance that they will be told about their students at the training session.

We have trained more than 50 tutors in a single session, but that has happened after a program has been running for many years. Smaller numbers are more realistic in the early stages of building a reading tutoring program: they allow for more individualized attention for the tutors. Even so, with the group work we incorporate into the training, it is preferable to have 10 to 12 tutors at a session. In the first years of a tutoring program, one is glad to have anyone! Tutoring programs are built one tutor at a time. With larger numbers of volunteers, schools must provide enough personnel to give assistance to small groups and to answer individual questions.

The structure of a viable training session, as outlined below, demonstrates that such a session should be as interactive as possible. Too often, training sessions become times of information overload, overwhelming novices. Tutors can absorb only a certain amount of information in a single session. Some information they really do not need to know at the beginning of tutoring—it can be shared through the ongoing communication between classroom teachers and tutors. The initial training session is one of those times when less is more.

The training session should be held at a time when classroom teachers, as well as tutors, are available. It should run between 1-1/2 to 2 hours after school or in the very early evening. The seating needs to be comfortable and allow for easy conversation and group work, as well as for the display of information using an overhead projector or a chalkboard. A classroom with movable furniture works just fine. Typically, we provide nourishment at training sessions: healthy snacks such as fruit, granola bars, water, and juice. People are encouraged to get food and drink on their arrival and again about halfway through the training.

We recommend providing name tags for each participant, including presenters, along with pencils and paper, school schedules, a map of the school, and a list of school personnel and their employment titles as well as teaching assignments (e.g., Salim Mangal, Grade 7 teacher). A professional tone is established if a pocket-folder is provided for each participant: the pockets provide a good place for tutors to keep the school information. We suggest putting a label on the front of each folder with the school board logo, the school name, address, and telephone number.

A sample agenda for a training session follows.

Sturgeon Falls Secondary School Reading Tutoring Program
Tutor Training Session
September 12, 2006, 4:00–5:45 pm

1. Welcome and introductions	5 minutes
2. Why tutoring is important at our school	5 minutes
3. Introducing the reading process	30 minutes
4. How tutors can get to know their students	10 minutes
5. Demonstrating ways to build confidence	10 minutes
6. Introducing the principles of effective tutoring	15 minutes
7. How to plan a good tutoring session	10 minutes
8. Introducing the tutoring binder	5 minutes
9. Closure: Reinforcing school support and the importance of establishing a positive relationship	5 minutes

---

1. Welcome and introductions

All participants introduce and say one thing about themselves. If more than 20 people are present, this activity should be done in small groups once school personnel have introduced themselves. This feature is important in establishing a sense of the larger tutoring community at the school and in valuing each tutor.

2. Why tutoring is important at our school

This brief, but compelling introduction to tutoring should refer to the diversity of ways of learning and the need of some students for one-to-one interaction. It should also provide a general description of the students who need tutoring support. Ideally, it would also honestly outline the school's overall literacy achievement and explain how the tutoring program will fill the needs of a targeted group of students. There should be an emphasis on how schools look to the wider community for support of student learning.

At the end, the introduction should emphasize the value that the school places on each individual person in the school and on the relationships that tutors develop with their students. These relationships and activities give hope to students, virtually all of whom blame themselves for being unable to read well.

Here is a good place to introduce the ways that the classroom teacher and the school support tutors. A handout might be distributed.

3. Introducing the reading process

Begin by asking volunteers to talk about their personal experiences with reading and learning how to read. Use these experiences to demonstrate that there is no single way to teach reading.

Many people who become reading tutors learned to read almost effortlessly. In order to help them understand the challenges faced by the people they will be tutoring, we often provide tutors with an introduction to reading, such as "About Reading: An Introduction" on page 21, and work with a text that is difficult to understand, such as "Ladle Rat Rotten Hut." (See Appendix 1 for the full text and translation.)

Demonstration: Once tutors hear a brief introduction to what reading is, they get into small groups and read "Ladle Rat Rotten Hut" (see text on page 22). After about five minutes, we stop the groups and give them the full title, "Ladle Rat Rotten Hut end der Wicket Woof." Within a few minutes, we show them an illustration of Little Red Riding Hood—choose one of several available in books. We ask what the story is and invite volunteers to read it. One workshop leader then reads the whole passage, with inflection to help listeners understand the text. We find that having the text on an overhead projector or as a PowerPoint presentation is helpful.

For many students, one of the most important aspects of the tutoring program is the fact that adults are taking time from their own lives and dedicating it to *them*—week after week. This fact reinforces that, although students may be struggling in school because of their reading, they are people of worth. Tutors need to know that this is how most students who are selected for tutoring feel. Teachers and principals are the ones to tell them.

About Reading: An Introduction

What is reading?

Reading is meaning making. It begins with decoding symbols, including letters, numbers, and figures, and making meaning from those symbols.

Reading a passage aloud with expression usually indicates comprehension and meaning making—but not always. Sometimes, it is possible to read a passage, understanding every individual word, but not relating those words to individual knowledge and experience. When this occurs, reading comprehension is low.

Reading every word correctly does matter, but it is not enough. Fluent readers link words into larger ideas and use the details to support the meaning they are constructing; when those individual words are not linked to the larger ideas, though, comprehension and meaning making suffer dramatically. That is why we distinguish between *decoding* and *comprehension*.

Expert reader practices

Expert readers already know a lot about what they are going to read before they begin the word-by-word reading process. Invariably, they have done many of the following things before doing what many people think of as "reading."

- They read the title and think about what they know in relation to the title.
- They preview the "big picture" and relate it to personal experience and knowledge.
- They look for additional clues on what the passage is about.
- They preview subheads or section titles, and look at pictures or graphs.
- They predict what the passage will say, something that helps activate memories and specific words associated with the given topic. This, in turn, helps make reading more fluent, and that supports construction of meaning, or comprehension.
- They review what they have read, which reinforces the reading and helps to internalize the new information.

This previewing can be done verbally or in writing. The advantage of writing is that it involves a different learning style—kinesthetic—thereby using another mental pathway to learning.

About Reading Levels

Students who need tutoring in reading will work at two different reading levels with their tutors.

The *independent reading level* is the level at which the student can read and comprehend without any help from a tutor. The student recognizes virtually all words and understands the content well. Text at this level could be viewed as easy.

The *instructional reading level* is the level at which the student requires help in recognizing words and comprehending text. Providing assistance with word strategies and recognition, the tutor will notice the greatest amount of growth at this level.

There is also the *frustrational reading level*, which is to be avoided. That is the level at which a student cannot make enough meaning of a text. Any student may resist reading material at this too difficult level.

Ladle Rat Rotten Hut

Wants pawn term, dare worsted ladle gull hoe lift witter murder inner ladle cordage honour itch offer louge, dock florist. Disc ladle gull orphan worry putty ladle rat hut, end for disc raisin pimple caulder Ladle Rat Rotten Hut.

Wan mourning Rat Rotten Hut's murder colder inset: "Ladle Rat Rotten Hut, heresy ladle basking insome burden barter and shirker cockles. Tisk disc ladle basking tudor cordage offer groin murder hoe lifts honour udder site offer florist. Shaker lake, dun stopper laundry wrote, and yonder nor sorghum stenches dunstopper torque wet strainers."

"Hoe-cake, Murder," resplendent Ladle Rat Rotten Hut, an tickle ladle basking on stuttered oft. Honour wrote tudor cordage offer groin murder, Ladle Rat Rotten Hut mitten a bag woof.

"Wail, wail, wail," set disc wicket woof, "evanescent Ladle Rat Rotten Hut! Wares or putty ladle gull goring wizard ladel basking?"

"Armor goring tumor groin murder's," reprisal ladle gull. "Grammar's seeking bet. Armor ticking arson burden barter and sirker cockles."

"Will, heifer blessing woke," setter wicket woof, butter taught tomb shelf: "Oil tickle shirt court tudor cordage offer groin murder. Oil ketchup wetter letter on, den . . . heh heh heh!"

Mural: Yonder nor sorghum stenches shut ladle gulls stopper torque wet strainers!

Source: From *Anguish Languish*, written by Prof. H. L. Chace in 1940

Brief discussion about reading as meaning making and about using cueing systems for making meaning follows. Here, tutors consider pragmatic cues, such as use of the title and use of an illustration. We stress that use of cueing systems is a mental habit that good readers do subconsciously—one of what we call *habits of mind*. We emphasize that over the course of the tutoring program, tutors will learn how to make these habits of mind visible to students and will reinforce these habits with students at every tutoring session.

Tutors are then introduced to a few more reading instruction concepts, such as decoding, comprehension, word recognition, and cueing systems—five in total. These are sufficient to provide the tutors with a framework to use in their tutoring sessions.

4. How tutors can get to get to know their students

Successful tutoring depends on a positive relationship between the learner and the tutor. The tutor must take time to get to know the learner's strengths, needs, and interests. Get acquainted activities for tutor and learner help build trust.

In pairs, tutors can interview each other to complete "All About Me" forms. (A student example appears in Chapter 4, page 48; the blank template is an appendix on page 139.) Tutors will later take these completed forms to their first tutoring session, sharing information about themselves with the students and working with the students to complete forms with student information.

5. Demonstrating ways to build confidence

Students who don't read well have lost confidence in themselves and their ability to become good readers. Tutors will need a repertoire of strategies to build confidence in their students. They will need to know how to begin where their learners are. By fostering early and ongoing success, they will learn how to increase confidence. Through regular, specific, and meaningful feedback, tutors will demonstrate growth and encourage future effort.

At the training session, distribute and discuss these handouts: "Ways to Build Student Confidence and Self-Esteem," Chapter 4, page 44, and "How to Provide Useful Feedback," Chapter 5, page 61.

The principles of effective tutoring are found in summary form in Chapter 5.

6. Introducing the principles of effective tutoring

Explicit instruction and strategic reading—modelling the habits of mind associated with successful reading. Discuss explicit instruction and strategic reading and the importance of tutors modelling and talking aloud about the things that they do as they read. Give an example of tutors modelling the talking aloud about their own reading (you could choose something from this book). Explain that tutors will develop this skill over time, with teacher support.

Goal setting. Discuss goal setting with tutors and give examples.

An emphasis on decoding and comprehension. Emphasize the reading processes of decoding and comprehension, noting that tutors will build more and more strategies to support students in these areas as the tutoring progresses. Distribute and discuss "Diagnostic Reading Assessment," page 57, and "Simple Diagnostic Reading Assessment," page 58.

Introduce the concepts of independent reading and instructional reading. (See Chapter 9 for a comparison.)

Planning for each tutoring session. Introduce the expectation of planning for each tutoring session, noting that the classroom teacher or tutoring coordinator will need to see a brief written plan. Discuss details of this next.

Brief written observations. Advise tutors to make brief written observations of their students at each session and to use these in planning the next tutoring sessions.

Communication. Emphasize that tutors need to be in touch with the classroom teacher or tutoring coordinator at every tutoring session.

7. How to plan a good tutoring session

Introduce the tutoring plan (see Chapter 4, page 51). Distribute a copy of the sample plan and take the tutors through it, stressing again that plans will take increasingly less time to write as the tutoring progresses. Remind tutors to talk with the classroom teacher about the plans and to expect the teacher to have strong suggestions for them.

After reviewing the sample, distribute blank copies of the form and advise tutors that they will be expected to follow this format for their plans.

Briefly discuss text selection. Emphasize the importance of finding texts at a level that the student finds easy for some of each tutoring session—the student's independent reading level—and for finding other texts at a harder reading level—or instructional level—for part of each tutoring session. Stress that although teachers and tutors look for books and other texts of interest at the right reading levels, they often do not quite hit the mark. Tutors should expect this and initially have about three texts with them as options. The initial uncertainty holds true for even the most experienced tutors when they first get to know new students. As tutors get to know their students, text selection becomes less problematic.

8. Introducing the tutoring binder

Advise tutors that they will need to use tutoring binders. A **tutoring binder** is a three-ring binder with tutoring plans, observations of the student, any forms completed, records, and samples of student work. For the training session, prepare and distribute a list of what the school expects to see in the tutoring binder and explain the binder's purposes:

- to provide information to the tutor for planning
- to provide information in a form that enables the classroom teacher to quickly and easily see what is happening in order to make suggestions and support the tutor
- to provide information for students to see their own growth and change over time
- to provide information for mid-tutoring and end-of-tutoring communication to parent/guardians

Tutors are expected to keep the binder up-to-date so that it can be used for these purposes.

9. Closure: Reinforce school support and the importance of establishing a positive relationship

By the end of the 90-minute training session, tutors may feel overwhelmed. Be sure to stress that the school knows tutors gain expertise over time, that the classroom teacher, librarian, and special education resource teacher are there for support, and that the single most important thing early on is to establish a positive relationship with the student.

Prepare Students for Tutoring

Students need to be prepared for tutoring sessions, too. Our research has found that tutoring works best when the students taking part in tutoring programs do so willingly. Teachers may well initiate the invitation or possibility of one-to-one tutoring, but students make the final decision on whether or not to participate.

Approaching students in a positive manner is important. For example, the teacher might say: "We're planning to start a free tutoring program in reading. There will be community volunteers working one-to-one with students, probably in the library. We're inviting the students whom we feel would benefit most to participate. Do you think you might be interested?"

Students are usually eager to receive this free tutoring, particularly in the second and subsequent years of a reading tutoring program at the school. Using an invitational approach ensures that students feel they have control over their lives; our experience shows that they are more likely to be committed to the program.

Participation in a tutoring program is not a right: it is a privilege. Through discussion, teachers should be sure to help students realize that they carry certain responsibilities for the success of the program. Some of these are outlined below.

- Students should be ready for each tutoring session, bringing any content-area reading materials that the teacher expects to be read and being mentally ready for the tutor and tutoring session.
- Students should recognize that tutors are volunteering personal time not only during the tutoring sessions, but in the preparation for those sessions.
- Students should let their tutors know the approaches that work best for them, as well as those that are not working.
- They should try to be patient, but let their tutors know when they are getting frustrated or tired.
- Students should always do their best.
- Students should celebrate their successes!

Create the Program Framework

Classroom teachers assume leadership and mentoring roles, as well as management roles in tutoring programs. They play a critical role both in identifying the students who will most benefit from tutoring (see Chapter 3) and also in supporting the tutoring initiative. First and foremost, they need to ensure open communication between teachers, students, parents/guardians, and the school principal.

We recommend that classroom teachers set certain expectations for themselves. Tutors need to know who their primary contact is, who will orient them to the school, and of whom they can ask questions throughout the program. It is recommended that teachers select salient points from the list below and make a handout that tutors can take with them. Any handout should also include the school telephone number and the name of the school secretary. Accepting several of the following teacher tasks will do much to ensure a successful school tutoring program:

- Be the primary contact person for the tutoring program.
- In consultation with various colleagues, such as the special education resource teacher, select students to be tutored; also, create a back-up list of students who might be tutored if initial students are absent.
- Create, distribute, and collect parent/guardian information and consent forms for participation of the students selected. (See the samples at the end of this chapter.)
- Arrange all the organizational aspects for the tutoring program (e.g., tutoring space, computers, and software) and inform the principal.
- Welcome tutors to the school and the classroom. Be sure to give them a tour of the school and to introduce them to the principal.
- Show them tutoring locations: these should be quiet spaces where students will not be distracted, but also open and public. School libraries often have spaces that are particularly effective.
- Give volunteers their tutoring timetables.
- Review general expectations of tutors, stressing the importance of their attendance, preparation for each tutoring session, and communication with the classroom teacher.
- Discuss learners' profiles and learning needs with tutors.
- Discuss diagnostic assessment of learners.
- Provide tutors with an initial opportunity to observe the classroom program. Doing this enables the tutors to understand academic expectations and level of independence expected at this grade level.
- Conduct a training session for the tutors, outlining the goals and expected tutoring plan. (In addition to the training session guidelines earlier in this chapter, teachers can copy parts of this book as a resource.)
- Arrange for the principal to explain the importance of maintaining personal boundaries, particularly in one-to-one teaching and learning situations.
- Collect the tutors' police screening checks, record whose police checks have been received, and file them according to school protocols.
- Share pertinent resources, strategies and general knowledge with the tutors throughout the tutoring program to support their efforts.
- Encourage creativity, initiative, and professionalism.
- Monitor, discuss, and provide informal feedback regarding the tutors' plans after the first session and thereafter on a weekly basis;

Program modifications may be needed to meet your local needs. The important thing is that teachers, students, and tutors clearly understand their roles, responsibilities, and expectations.

track attendance of tutors, and provide materials whenever possible.

- Should any concern arise, first discuss the situation openly and frankly with the tutor. If the concern regards the students being tutored, work with other school personnel and the students themselves to resolve the concern; if the concern regards the tutor, recognize that tutors may not know or understand school protocols or policy.
- If students are being tutored during class time, be prepared for students to be absent from class. Give them homework at the beginning of class, ask class partners to take notes for students being tutored, and release students from class on time.
- Later on in the program, review drafts of tutor reports to parents, receive final drafts of these reports, and ensure that the reports are sent to students' homes, retaining copies for school records.
- At the end of the program, arrange a gesture of appreciation for tutors. Ideally, the acknowledgment would involve the principal in some way, for example, the principal's signature on a thank-you letter or on a certificate of appreciation.

If more than one teacher in a school is involved in a tutoring program, some of these responsibilities should be allocated to a single person who coordinates the program for the school.

Involve Parents or Guardians and Keep Them Informed

Before tutoring begins, parents or guardians of the students to be tutored need written information about the program, as well as consent forms. If they are not fluent in English, regular school protocols regarding communication should be followed: letters may need to be translated so that they fully understand. Pages 31 and 32 show a sample letter and consent form.

Once students are in a tutoring program, effective teachers will ensure that parents and guardians are kept informed of their progress. We recommend communication after the first four or five weeks and again at the ten-week time mark. If the tutoring continues past ten weeks, a third and final letter should be written, signalling the end of the tutoring. Best practice is for the tutor to prepare all letters, showing an initial draft of the report to the classroom teacher and then submitting a final draft. The classroom teacher saves a copy of the report for school records and sends the original home to the parents.

Our research and experience show that parents and guardians of students who participate in school tutoring programs are extremely supportive and grateful for the one-to-one attention their children are receiving. They speak of the engagement of their children, their desire for the tutoring to continue, their deep appreciation for the skill development that occurs, and also of the clear message given by the tutors that their children are treated as persons of value.

Establish Communication Mechanisms

Tutoring calls for much on-the-spot decision making and, given the position of trust that tutors gain, it often involves receiving information that other school personnel may or may not know. Without communication of insights and professional knowledge from the classroom teacher, tutors may feel isolated and uncomfortable about the decisions they are making and the information they are receiving from their students.

Determining in advance the type and timing of communication between tutors and teachers is important. People usually *intend* to communicate, but busy lives and school realities often interfere. We strongly recommend that regular communication mechanisms be established. Although communication does not always have to be face to face, periodic face-to-face communication is important.

Tutors and classroom teachers have found a variety of communication mechanisms to be effective at different times in the tutoring program. Mechanisms include the following:

Canvas bag: For use every tutoring session, a canvas bag can be hung in the teacher's classroom where it is easily accessible to tutors. Even with multiple tutors, classroom teachers can readily leave notes and tutoring materials for individual tutors at their own convenience, such as after school. In this way, tutors can be alerted to achievements or challenges that students have had. In turn, tutors can write brief notes, perhaps one- or two-sentence comments about the day's tutoring, making reference to specific skills or the successful use of specific resources or activities.

Wire basket: Alternatively, a wire basket or plastic tub could be placed in an easily accessible location. Teachers and tutors could use it in similar ways to the canvas bag; however, this option does not ensure the kind of confidentiality that the bag affords.

Face-to-face meetings: Every three or four weeks, at a meeting scheduled in advance, tutors and teachers should review learner needs, goals and strategies, and resources being used. The purpose of these meetings is to discuss student progress, including work students have done during the tutoring. The tutoring binder is a key item for this meeting. It enables classroom teachers to see the specifics they need in order to make informed suggestions for the next three or four weeks of tutoring.

The first of these meetings also allows teachers to observe tutors, gain a tangible sense of what is occurring in tutoring sessions, give concrete suggestions to tutors, and report specifics to parents and guardians during parent–teacher interviews. Unless the tutor requests it or the student says something that suggests an additional observation might be helpful, this type of meeting need not occur more than once.

Letters written by tutors: As previously agreed, after four or five weeks of tutoring, tutors draft letters to their students' parents or guardians summarizing activities and progress to date. Classroom teachers edit the drafts and within a week, final versions are sent home and copies kept for school files. (Chapter 5 provides a model.)

At the end of tutoring, after 10 or 11 weeks, tutors write either final letters to the parents or good-bye letters to the students, with copies to the parents. The same format and protocols are followed as above.

Provide Tutoring Resources

Classroom teachers need to ensure that tutors know the level at which their students are reading and at least initially, give tutors texts at the right reading level for use in their tutoring sessions. On the other hand, tutors need to search for and bring in texts intended to appeal to the students they are tutoring.

Finding resources for tutoring is a shared responsibility. Teachers and tutors should discuss the topic regularly, particularly in their face-to-face meetings. Classroom teachers have expertise in grade level, content area, and age-appropriate texts; however, they may not know of specific texts at the grade level needed for students being tutored—all of whom are reading below grade-level expectations and some of whom are reading far below grade-level expectations. Sleuthing by the tutor may turn up instructional level texts on a content-area topic or topic of interest to the student. Or it may be that teachers have a bank of resources that span reading levels on a given topic either related to content being taught or to students' interests. Only in recent years have many of these resources become available, and more are coming onto the market all the time; however, neither teacher nor tutor should make assumptions that the other can locate the needed resources.

For the initial tutoring sessions, it is particularly important for teachers to give tutors resources at the appropriate reading level. Novice tutors do not know about or have access to the kinds of resources that teachers do; at this stage, they will also not know how to identify resources at the appropriate reading level. The canvas bag, noted above, provides an easy way to exchange resources. The time period for which the materials are available should be noted.

Chapter 9 addresses the issues of resources in some detail.

It may be helpful to refer tutors to the school's special education teacher and the librarian for resources. Perhaps the easiest way for tutors to first make contact with these people is to write quick notes to set up meetings to inquire about tutoring resources. Classroom teachers should encourage tutors to take this kind of initiative and be sure to alert special education teachers and librarians that tutors may be doing this. In addition, classroom teachers will want to make note of particularly effective resources that tutors have found or created. Ideally, this information would be shared with the school librarian and kept on file for future use.

Enable Tutors to Function Properly Within the School

For many volunteers, this will be the first school tutoring experience. They will not know about rigorous protocols governing interaction between professionals or para-professionals and students. In the initial meeting with tutors, the school needs to inform volunteers about setting personal boundaries.

The issue is one of tutor vulnerability, if only by perception. Teacher unions are well aware of teacher vulnerability regarding professional boundaries; tutors are vulnerable, too, as, by definition, they are placed in positions where they are alone with a student, where they are encouraged to establish and maintain a position of trust, and often where they are chosen by the student as a confidant regarding personal issues. As one union states, "A caring professional relationship always helps a student to learn. But this relationship has boundaries of time, place, purpose and activity" (Elementary Teachers Federation of Ontario: www.etfo. on.ca).

In order to protect everyone, the school must educate tutors about personal boundaries. Given the seriousness of the issue, the principal may wish to conduct this information session or may allocate this responsibility to another school administrator. Ideally, this issue would be dealt with at a second and much briefer training session, lasting about one-half hour and focusing just on school codes and policies, including personal boundaries between students and all adults working with them. This training could occur before or after a tutoring session in the first week or two of tutoring.

Issues of student and staff safety have prompted the creation of procedures and policies that are much more formalized than in the past. In order to become functioning members of the school community, tutors need to be familiar with school dress and behavior codes and school policies. If schools do not tell tutors about their policies, tutors will be unable to function appropriately. School handbooks, fire and safety procedures, and procedures for reporting absence or off-site activities are examples of the kinds of information that all school volunteers need to know.

Tutors need to know school, board, and legal procedures for reporting suspected abuse, too. They are in a position of trust, are older than the students they are tutoring, and are at a certain distance from them. They work from an ethic of care and concern and are prime people for disclosure. They need to know what to do with any disclosure they are given—and what their legal responsibilities are in this regard. This information would be covered in the second training session.

Show Appreciation of Tutors

It is important for schools to show appreciation of all volunteers working with their students. It is also the right thing to do. This appreciation need not be extravagant, but does need to reflect the appreciation of the school principal as the official school representative. A simple thank-you letter or a certificate of appreciation with a handshake delivered by the principal sets a tone for everyone involved. It reminds tutors and teachers alike that educating children and supporting all learners is a responsibility and privilege of the whole community. We recommend thanking volunteers publicly, either at a staff meeting or at a lunchtime event designed specifically to show appreciation to them.

This simple kind of appreciation will keep tutors coming back, which is what schools need. It does not take many years for a school to build a cadre of trained and deeply committed volunteers, all of whom hone their skills over the years and help support all youth to fulfill their potential. Now, isn't *that* a grand idea!

Examples of an information letter for parents or guardians and a consent form appear on pages 31 and 32.

Reading Tutoring Program: Information Letter

[School Letterhead]

September 2006

Dear Ms. King,

Your son Roderick has been recommended to take part in a free reading tutoring program, conducted by volunteer tutors, and he has indicated that he would like to do this.

The tutors will be providing one-to-one tutoring based on the learning style preferences and interests of each student. Tutors have been trained by us and have also had background screening checks. Tutoring will be individualized to student needs and learning style preferences and may incorporate computer technology as well as face-to-face tutoring. All tutors will work under the direction of the classroom teacher.

The tutoring will run from October through December. Your child will be withdrawn from class twice a week to be tutored during regular school hours for 45 minutes each session.

If you are in agreement with having Roderick take part in this tutoring program, please sign the attached consent form and return it by September 22 to your child's teacher.

If you have any questions, please call me or get in touch with Roderick's teacher at 123-456-7777.

Sincerely,

T. Mangal

T. Mangal, Principal

Reading Tutoring Participation Consent Form

[School Letterhead]

September 2006

I have read the letter of information about the Reading Tutoring Program being conducted at Sturgeon Falls Secondary School and any questions have been answered to my satisfaction.

I am aware that my child's participation is voluntary and that I may choose to stop my child's participation at any time. I understand that information will be kept confidential and that the tutor will be working with my child's classroom teacher to identify needs and effective approaches. If I have any questions or concerns, I know that I can contact any of the people indicated on the information letter.

I agree that my child ___Roderick___ may participate in the Reading Tutoring Program which will commence in October 2006 and run through December 2006.

My signature below also indicates that I have received a copy of this consent form.

Student's full name: ___Roderick King___
(Please print.)

Name of parent/guardian: ___Janine King___
(Please print.)

Signature: ___Janine A. King___

Date: ___September 15, 2006___

**Please return this form to your child's teacher by
Friday, September 22, 2006.**

Chapter 3 Working with Dependent Readers

Teachers set the tone for how tutors work with students being tutored, so it is essential to convey that these students are, above all, individuals with talents, interests, and strengths. Recognizing this is especially important since students themselves may feel that their weakness in reading overshadows their gifts and talents in other areas. Many terms have traditionally been used to describe students who have difficulty with reading: *slow, struggling, remedial, disadvantaged, at risk,* just to name a few. Such labels are often accompanied by a long list of negative behaviors, such as these:

- a poor attitude to reading
- a lack of willingness to try a new text
- a sense of personal failure
- inconsistent performance
- difficulty remembering what they have learned
- weak organizational skills
- use of avoidance strategies
- difficulty staying on task
- lack of concentration

When tutors first meet the students they will be tutoring, they will likely encounter some of these behaviors. The problem with this list, although accurate, is its emphasis on the negative. If tutors focus on these behaviors, they risk constructing learners in these ways and missing *the persons* with whom they will be working, persons with strengths, interests, hopes, and fears.

Teachers need to properly orient tutors serving any of their students. It is important for tutors to understand that any negative characteristics that may be present are likely a reflection of underlying challenges faced by the learners. After years of frustration with reading, some students may have acquired negative attitudes and experience a sense of personal failure and lack of self-worth. These attitudes should not be surprising.

Especially in tutoring situations, though, using labels with mainly negative connotations should be avoided. The danger is that they lead to a deficit model of instruction, one that assumes something is wrong with the learner. If tutors develop this perspective, they may assume that their job is to figure out the cause of students' problems and then find a way to "fix" them. This way of thinking is far from desirable.

Identify Dependent Readers

A more positive approach has been suggested by Beers (2003). She makes a compelling argument for considering the extent to which someone is able to use effective reading strategies as the basis for determining who needs help. She differentiates between two kinds of readers: *independent* and *dependent*. These terms are more neutral than talking about good and poor readers, and they carry the sense of student development, from being dependent readers to becoming more and more independent in their reading.

Independent readers have at their disposal a wide range of strategies that they can use successfully when encountering a new text. It is from these ranks that tutors come. **Dependent readers**, on the other hand, have a limited repertoire of strategies available to them. For one reason or another, they have not yet acquired the strategies used by independent readers. These include the following:

- drawing from a bank of sight words at their disposal
- knowing how to decode new words
- using context to figure out what new words mean
- reading with expression
- reading at a speed adequate to obtain meaning from a text
- rereading to clarify meaning
- predicting what is likely to happen next
- asking and answering questions about a text
- making inferences
- drawing conclusions
- making generalizations
- setting a purpose for reading, whether it be for enjoyment or to gain information
- recalling information from a text
- using features of a text, such as subheads or margin comments, to aid comprehension

This type of strategy-based approach to teaching reading is most conducive to effective tutoring. As successful readers, tutors already have a wide variety of effective reading strategies at their disposal. They may not always be conscious of these strategies, at least not initially, but as good readers, they have learned how to use them well. As a result, they are excellent role models for dependent readers. One of the best ways in which they can help their learners is to model the strategies that they use with ease and confidence.

Students struggle with reading for a variety of reasons, so clumping them all under one superficial label does not help the teacher or the tutor in planning instruction to address specific learning needs. In this chapter, we explore some of the most common types of learners that teachers refer for tutoring. These types include kinesthetic learners, learners for whom English is a second or additional language, and those with a learning disability. In each case, a typical profile is presented and discussed, and the implications for tutoring addressed. Once tutors understand or determine which strategies learners have at their disposal and which ones they

The general tutoring strategies explained in Chapters 6, 7, and 8 are recommended for all kinds of dependent readers. Beyond that, specific strategies that have proven to be effective for tutoring each of the three kinds of learners discussed here are presented in the appendixes. These may be photocopied and given to tutors as appropriate.

do not, they will be able to build upon what the students know in a positive and constructive manner.

Independent Versus Instructional Reading Levels

Although dependent readers are not meeting grade-level expectations, they can read some texts completely on their own and gain enjoyment from them. These texts are said to be at the student's **independent reading level**. Texts at a student's independent reading level are used for introduction of new skills and concepts, reinforcement, motivation, and enjoyment. They are often used to introduce the *habits of mind* that students are learning—the reading habits of successful readers—as well as strategies that may initially appear to be more difficult for a particular student. In this way, the content or skill that students have mastered is used to support the introduction of more difficult content or skills.

At other times, texts that students are unable to read by themselves are used. As long as students can read the texts with some support, the texts are said to be at the student's **instructional reading level**. These texts are used for different instructional purposes, namely, to apply and reinforce reading habits of mind and strategies that have been previously introduced.

Oftentimes, students get fatigued when working with instructional level reading materials. Tutors need to anticipate this and be sensitive to student fatigue. When fatigue seems to be setting in, effective tutors support their students in completing the task at hand. They might share the task, scribe or write for students, or simplify the task.

A text may be at one student's independent reading level and another student's instructional level. Oftentimes, even experienced teachers cannot determine when a text might be too difficult for a student. The important thing is to be sensitive to student fatigue and frustration; when either becomes apparent, the tutor should step in to help the student complete the task at hand.

Supporting Kinesthetic Learners

Shawn: Profile of a kinesthetic learner

Shawn is a very active fourteen-year-old. In the winter, he loves snowboarding. During most summer days, he can be found at the local skateboarding park practising his skills. In school, he is popular with his classmates and polite to his teachers; he just never seems to be able to complete anything he starts. In his Grade 10 English class, he is happy to leaf through comic books and sports magazines for brief periods of time. When it comes to full-length books, however, he would much rather talk to his buddies about what they're going to do after school. Sitting still for any length of time is impossible for him, especially if it involves reading and writing.

Shawn is in a constant state of motion. He talks with his hands, finds the most creative excuses to get up out of his seat, and is always the first to volunteer to bring the attendance sheet to the office. This year he has found his niche in drama, for which he has a real flair. Unfortunately, improvisation and mime will not help

Like most kinesthetic learners, Shawn was initially wary about the tutoring; however, he agreed to try it and warmed up to his tutor within a few sessions. The genuine interest his tutor showed in him and the tutoring approaches that drew on his kinesthetic strength—for example, planning three or four breaks during the tutoring for Shawn to get up and move around or using prefix and root word cards for Shawn to create new words—quickly made Shawn enthusiastic about his tutoring sessions.

him pass the literacy test he needs for graduation. In the past, he has always gotten by on his physical talents and natural charm, but for the first time in his school life, these attributes are not enough. Shawn realizes that he must get help with his reading if he is going to graduate and get into an applied arts program at his local community college.

Kinesthetic students learn best through hands-on approaches: ones that allow them to actively explore the physical world around them. If kinesthetic learners can touch and experience what they are learning, they will process and remember information much more readily than if they read it or hear it. Acting, pantomiming, recording what they read, and using manipulatives as part of the reading process are approaches that will greatly increase their chances of success. The strengths of kinesthetic students include the ability to recall experiences they have had, to rehearse instructions, and to learn while they are active. They enjoy assembling and disassembling things, role-playing, and participating actively.

Implications for Tutoring Kinesthetic Learners

A large number of students who need help with reading, especially among boys, are kinesthetic learners. Tutors of kinesthetic learners need to be aware of their learners' needs for the following:

"Strategies for Tutoring Kinesthetic Learners," on pages 132–33, is a reproducible list of specific tutoring strategies that address the needs of kinesthetic learners.

- tutoring approaches that involve physical activity
- concrete, hands-on materials
- ways to help them release extra energy
- learning approaches that involve oral language
- well-planned and carefully timed lessons
- frequent breaks and changes in activities
- use of the computer when possible

Supporting Students with English as a Second or Additional Language

Mallalai: Profile of a learner for whom English is new

Mallalai is fifteen years old. She and her family have recently arrived from Afghanistan. After many difficult years in their homeland, her parents have decided to begin a new life in North America. Both of Mallalai's parents are well educated, but because girls were not allowed to go to school during the Taliban years, she has not learned how to read, even in her native language. As she starts school in her new country and encounters English for the first time, she must learn to read from the beginning. That letters have sounds is still a mystery to her. Mallalai is overwhelmed by print text, and the concepts that letters have names, make sounds and form words are new to her. Mallalai is highly motivated, however. She is determined to learn to read as soon as possible. She is also fortunate to have parents who are very supportive.

Students who lack basic understanding of reading principles in their first language usually need additional support in learning letter–sound correspondences and then in combining sounds to make words. Tutors need to explicitly ensure that students understand and use basic English reading strategies, such as left-to-right progression.

Many students whose first language is not English will benefit from a tutoring program. Most of these students have a strong understanding of basic reading principles and are able to use them quite effectively in their first language. For instance, even if word order is different in English than in their first language, they will already have internalized the idea that word order follows a limited number of patterns and that knowing something about those patterns assists in reading. For the few, like Mallalai, who have not yet acquired basic literacy levels in their first language, the instructional approaches and strategies will need to be adapted.

Many students who are learning English as a new language are also learning about a new culture. Most texts, though, involve culturally specific references of which first language speakers are unaware: that is because they have deeply internalized cultural norms. It would be very helpful for classroom teachers to raise this with tutors before tutoring begins, reminding them to incorporate talk about cultural specifics as part of the tutoring.

Cultural references in texts may interfere with students' attempts to make meaning. For instance, a student may not understand that some soft drink companies pay money for recycling their glass bottles. Text reference to teens conducting a bottle drive to raise money would carry no meaning to the reader.

Students who are learning English as a new language will benefit when tutors keep a constant awareness of this interference. The successful tutor becomes a cultural guide as well as a reading support. In turn, students can teach their tutors about their own cultures, gaining in self-confidence and self-esteem while doing so. Most students learning English, though, will not volunteer this kind of information unless encouraged to do so.

> For students learning English as a second or additional language, effective tutors serve as cultural guides.

Implications for Tutoring Learners for Whom English Is a Second or Additional Language

Since students who are learning a new language will be at various stages of development, it is critical to determine individual student needs before tutoring begins. Some essential needs that tutors may encounter in these students are identified in the checklist that follows. It would be helpful if the teacher uses this checklist as a brief inventory of needs before tutoring begins.

Possible Needs of Students Learning English as a Second Language: A Checklist

Students who are learning English as a second or additional language may have tutoring needs in any of these areas:

- ❏ Recognizing the relationship between the sounds of the English language and the letters of the alphabet
- ❏ Learning basic vocabulary common to the school and community environment
- ❏ Recognizing and learning frequently used words found in most texts
- ❏ Learning how to apply basic reading strategies, such as sight recognition, phonics, using context clues to derive meaning from texts
- ❏ Understanding short, simple phrases and sentences
- ❏ Beginning to acquire subject-specific vocabulary
- ❏ Recognizing the main idea and key information in simple passages
- ❏ Developing fluency with simple passages
- ❏ Developing the habit of reading for enjoyment and information
- ❏ Using reading strategies to derive meaning from texts (e.g., recognizing cueing systems and word families, predicting, inferring, rereading)
- ❏ Learning how to locate information in textbooks and other resources by using tables of contents, headings, margin notes, indexes, glossaries, and photographs
- ❏ Beginning to read aloud, with fluency and appropriate phrasing and rhythm
- ❏ Choosing books and reading them with assistance or independently for a variety of purposes, including personal enjoyment
- ❏ Skimming and scanning texts for key information
- ❏ Beginning to use vocabulary acquisition strategies such as the following:
  - Recognizing how adding a prefix or suffix changes the meaning of a word
  - Hypothesizing about the meaning of unfamiliar words from context
  - Using a dictionary to check meaning and identifying parts of speech
  - Comparing main ideas and key information from a variety of sources

Note: Adapted from *English as a Second Language and English Literacy Development: A Resource Guide, 2001*, Ontario Ministry of Education

"Strategies for Tutoring Students for Whom English Is a Second or Additional Language," on pages 134–35, is a reproducible list of specific tutoring strategies to help students.

Selecting texts on familiar topics will greatly benefit students learning English as a second or additional language: they will be able to use prior knowledge to learn English words and phrases for familiar concepts. Similarly, it is a good idea for tutors to suggest that learners teach the context and terms of a topic in their own first language—tutors will get a better view of their learners as persons of value with things to teach them. As well as being fun and an opportunity to learn more about the learners' heritage culture(s), this sharing builds a stronger tutoring relationship and provides more motivation.

Supporting Students with Learning Disabilities

Brandon: Profile of a student with a learning disability

By the time they are adolescents, most students with learning disabilities have lived with others' frustration and blame for many years. These students often feel very frustrated by the challenges that their learning disabilities cause them and often have subconsciously perfected strategies to avoid failure. Tutors need to have patience and persistence, use encouragement and praise liberally, and celebrate success.

For Brandon, reading is a painful experience. Although he is articulate, good at sports, and popular with his peers, his reading level seems at a plateau. Intelligence tests indicate that Brandon has above-average ability for his age group, yet he has fallen further and further behind his classmates throughout the years of elementary schooling. Now that he is in Grade 7, Brandon is an angry and frustrated young man. Constantly in fights, he has started to bully some of the younger students in the school. He is often sent to the office for disruptive behavior. His homeroom teacher has remarked on Brandon's remarkable range of avoidance strategies: he constantly needs to go to the bathroom; his pencil always needs sharpening; and what is happening on the other side of the window is always more fascinating than what can be found between the covers of a book. When his science teacher introduces new vocabulary orally, Brandon has difficulty putting the sounds and syllables together to make complete words. In history, his rate of reading is so slow that by the time he gets to the bottom of the page, he has forgotten what was at the top. Reading a novel in language arts is a never-ending ordeal. Homework, especially anything that includes assigned readings from a textbook, is rarely completed. Brandon lives in constant fear that one of his teachers will ask him to read out loud. He is convinced that he will never make it to high school.

The Learning Disabilities Association of Canada (LDAC) begins its definition of learning disabilities in this way:

"Learning Disabilities" refer to a number of disorders which may affect the acquisition, organization, retention, understanding or use of verbal or nonverbal information. These disorders affect learning in individuals who otherwise demonstrate at least average abilities essential for thinking and/or reasoning. As such, learning disabilities are distinct from global intellectual deficiency.

Learning disabilities result from impairments in one or more processes related to perceiving, thinking, remembering or learning. These include, but are not limited to: language processing; phonological processing; visual spatial processing; processing speed; memory and attention; and executive functions (e.g. planning and decision-making).

Source: This definition, with its full text in the Appendixes, has been printed with permission from www. ldac.ca, the official Web site of the Learning Disabilities Association of Canada, Ottawa, Ontario.

This definition indicates that persons with learning disabilities often exhibit a significant discrepancy between their intellectual abilities and their performance in school.

Implications for Tutoring Students with Learning Disabilities

Students with learning disabilities have diverse needs in coping with school subjects that involve reading, writing, and mathematics. They often require support in general academic skills, such as organization and note making, and in the area of social relations (Weber and Bennett 2004).

In reading, tutors need to know what challenges students with learning disabilities face and that their role is to support their students in areas such as these:

- keeping their place in the text
- providing carefully thought-out answers to comprehension questions
- obtaining accurate meaning from a text
- acquiring effective strategies for determining the meanings of new words
- using context clues to determine meaning
- avoiding letter reversals, such as reading *was* for *saw*
- sequencing events in stories or processes
- making inferences
- recounting details
- acquiring a bank of common sight words
- improving their spelling

Attention to this kind of detail in reading is critical for all students being tutored, but particularly true for students with learning disabilities.

Our research has shown that regardless of learning style preference, boys become much more engaged with text when they work from areas of interest and use computers. Part of the tutor's responsibility, then, is to find texts of interest to learners and to help them connect the text they are reading to personal areas of interest.

"Strategies for Tutoring Students with Learning Disabilities," on pages 136–37, provides specific tutoring strategies to help students with reading.

The Prevalence of Kinesthetic Learners

Of several types of learners, the three types presented here—kinesthetic, those who are learning English as a second or additional language, and those with learning disabilities—most commonly experience difficulty in reading. Our research shows that of students selected for tutoring in Grades 7 to 10, about half were kinesthetic learners: people who need to be moving themselves or objects, touching things, and physically experiencing what they are learning. If tutors do not know where to begin in their tutoring, they would be well advised to choose kinesthetic activities and to model their own reading strategies, making their reading habits of mind visible to the students they are tutoring.

Chapter 4 Getting Off to a Good Start

A successful tutoring program reflects careful planning, creative improvisation, and empathic relationship building between tutors and learners. To ensure a good start for tutoring, teachers create or promote the following:

- a positive learning environment
- the building of learner self-esteem
- opportunities for tutors to get to know their students
- creation of an effective tutoring plan

Ensuring a Positive Learning Environment

A key ingredient for a successful start to tutoring is to create a positive atmosphere, one in which students feel comfortable and able to take risks, and tutors communicate a desire to help, not judge. There are several ways to help create such a learning environment.

Provide a quiet, safe work area for tutoring. Busy rooms, overcrowded areas, constant interruptions, and loud talk nearby are distractions that will make students uncomfortable. Students need to feel safe, free from distraction, comfortable, and listened to. The library often provides an ideal location, particularly at tables that are not in the main traffic area or in seminar rooms with windows. If an assigned location proves not to be distraction-free, tutors should bring that to the attention of the classroom teacher and find alternative locations.

Encourage informal chat at the beginning of tutoring time. The time before tutoring begins is important for chatting. Five minutes of informal "catching up" before each session starts sets a positive tone and allows tutors to be empathic and supportive of students *as persons*. This chat often gives insight into what might be more—or less!—successful that day and allows students to focus on the formal tutoring when it begins.

A cautionary note: Tutors should be aware that this early chatting time needs to be kept to an appropriate length. Some students may try to prolong the talking to avoid the hard work of reading.

Provide motivation. Tutors need to vary the presentation of the work to make it interesting. Perhaps they could use photos to generate discussion

Given the time it takes to find information, the Internet initiative will be realistic only if the tutor and student will be working on the same content-area topic for several weeks.

or PowerPoint slides that contain the day's readings. Teachers need to communicate with tutors about materials that they can provide. Conversely, if the classroom teacher does not have materials and the tutor is working on content-area reading, the tutor may be able to find materials on the Internet.

Perhaps students could be asked to teach tutors a skill of their own after reading a passage or students could play a game of finding tutor mistakes. Students delight in this, possibly because it puts the tutor into their shoes, as a person who not only makes mistakes, but also gets caught making mistakes. When they realize that mistake finding can be a strong learning activity, many tutors make deliberate mistakes, and when students catch them, express sentiments like, "You are certainly on your toes today!" Choice of reading materials should reflect student interests—specialty magazines may be important motivators. Sometimes, these materials may be found in the school library: tutors should be reminded to ask the librarian for assistance. More often, though, tutors supply these materials themselves, finding magazines and other popular culture texts that have articles on topics of student interest. Teacher acknowledgment of the extra effort is much appreciated by tutors.

Value regular attendance. Tutoring is a commitment, and as such, tutors must be sure to inform their students and tutoring coordinators of any upcoming absences well in advance of the dates. Tutors may be surprised to learn that if they are absent, students invariably think that the tutors no longer care about them or that they have done something to displease the tutors. Inevitably, students lose motivation. As damaging, however, is the student perception that the tutor represents another person who tried to help them, but decided that they were not worth the effort. Teachers are wise to communicate this to the tutors, for the sentiment is common to struggling readers—they blame themselves for their inability to read.

Respond to students with flexibility. Student performance will probably vary from session to session. If students are tired, over-excited, or getting over an illness, tutors should feel comfortable about refocusing the tutoring sessions on enjoyable and successful reading tasks. Doing some easy reading may be more motivating than any extensive instruction.

Provide opportunities for students to self-correct. Starting at the training session, tutors need to be told of the importance of students finding their own errors. Particularly in the first weeks of tutoring, teachers do well to reinforce this—inexperienced tutors have a strong urge to "correct." If, however, students do not find their own mistakes at the end of a sentence, and if those mistakes interfere with the meaning, tutors should draw attention to the errors. They might say, "Do you think these two words are the same?" or "Have a look at this again." Often, humor is a great relief for students. A comment such as, "It took a long time for you to make a mistake, but I *think* I may have caught you this time" may work with the student. It is wise to offer help if it appears needed, but tutors should give it only if wanted: students are more likely to remember something if they correct themselves.

Ensure that tasks are tied to student abilities. If the student is having a real struggle with a task, the task should be simplified. Sometimes, a task must be abandoned during a specific tutoring session, but it is preferable to modify the task so that the student can complete it successfully. Abandoning a task sends a message that the student is not a good enough reader or a smart enough person; completing a task sends a "can do" message and reinforces positive self-concept, confidence, and self-esteem. Tutors might share the task, reduce the number of examples, or offer to scribe responses given orally if students are getting fatigued.

As always, tutors need to be sensitive to the fact that students will feel that their shortcoming is the problem. When modifying a task, it is important to say something like, "This approach does not match your learning style preference very well. Let's try this in another way. Let me know if this approach works better for you." In their face-to-face meetings with tutors, teachers might provide specific words for tutors to use.

Apply focusing strategies, as needed. Tutors become responsible for helping students to stay focused. Here are some strategies to adopt:

- taking frequent breaks
- having students set their own goals
- letting students set how long they want to read (but suggesting reading as partners if the time set is too long)
- teaching relaxation techniques and doing them together, for example: standing and stretching; closing one's eyes and thinking of an image that makes one feel calm, such as a field bathed in sunshine, and breathing deeply and slowly 10 times; or tightening muscles, such as one's fist and arm, holding for a count of 10, and then slowly releasing the muscles, focusing on the feelings of relaxation that follow
- letting students fiddle with stress balls or tap pencils on their arms while reading
- working together with students to solve the focus problem

Building Student Self-Esteem

By the time dependent readers reach the middle school years, they may have accumulated a lot of negative feelings about reading and about themselves. In a world of print, they are constantly reminded that their lack of reading skills makes them different from their peers.

Dependent readers may suffer some of these negative feelings during tutoring. From their perspective, even meeting with a tutor requires a willingness to take a risk and open up, again, to possible failure. Many of them will have already received well-intentioned help that did not work. As a result, they may be skeptical about the tutoring being offered.

On the other hand, tutors represent hope. Nothing improves self-concept like success. Teachers need to emphasize that the tutors' task is not only to help students read better, but to build their self-confidence through successful experiences. The two are interdependent.

Here are some suggestions that teachers might make to tutors to help ensure learner success and build self-esteem.

Ways to Build Student Confidence and Self-Esteem

Accept students as they are, not as you wish them to be.

For example, if a student is fidgety and not concentrating, take a break: go for a short walk with the student or do some brief stretching exercises together.

Start at a level that the student has already mastered.

Begin the tutoring session by ensuring student success in the first activity. Either have the student reread familiar passages and praise increased fluency, or introduce new material that is of special interest to the student and at a comfortable reading level.

If a task proves to be too difficult, simplify it.

Do this in a way that allows the student to save face and ensures task completion. For instance, you might say: "How about taking turns on the next questions? You answer one, then I'll answer one." Or you might offer to scribe answers that the student gives orally.

Seek out and comment on strengths; then, be sure to build on them.

You might say: "You identified the main ideas really well! Let's work from that to identify just a few important details for each."

Use student suggestions to plan lessons.

You might say, "You talked about your interest in the planes used in the Second World War. Let's see if there might be a way we could incorporate that into the assignment you are working on for history."

Be aware of your own body language, facial expression, and tone of voice: keep them positive.

Leaning forward, making eye contact, and keeping your tone positive are all important ways of connecting with students, keeping them focused, and maintaining momentum. A smile is a great reinforcement technique and easy to use!

Ask students to work with you in finding answers.

Tutors do not always know the answer and that is just fine. When this happens, you gain a chance to model how to find answers. As always, talking aloud models the thinking process. For instance, you might say: "Hmmm. This question is asking us to name the patterns in physical geography. Is there anything in the text that will help us find those?"

Engage in reading experiences related to students' lives.

Research reaffirms time and again that students need to engage in reading activities that relate to their lives and their interests. The initial "All About Me" profile and the ongoing conversations between tutors and students are gold mines for topics and types of texts that students will find compelling. For instance, a student who is a young mother will find a pamphlet on parenting engaging and important. Or a student who wants to get his driver's licence will appreciate reading a driver education manual as part of his tutoring program. Such texts offer rich conversation and compelling material for learning the *habits of mind* associated with independent reading. They will also reinforce the value of reading.

Compare students' progress with how they were at the beginning, not against any other students.

For instance, you might ask the student to read aloud 200 to 300 words early in September and use a simple diagnostic reading assessment, noting the date, areas of strength, and areas needing attention. At the end of October, have the student do another read-aloud and then compare the latter reading to the earlier, noting areas of improvement and also planning areas on which to focus next.

Remind students of their growth every day.

Students need to be reminded of their progress at every tutoring session, not just once every four to six weeks. Informal comments during reading or at the end of the tutoring session go a long way to help students feel that they are making progress. You might say something like, "Wow! When I think back over today's session, you were able to do something you've never done before: read a whole passage from the history text completely on your own. Congratulations! Your work is really paying off!"

Ways to Get to Know Students

Although teachers will have invaluable information for tutors, it is also important for tutors to collect as much information about their students as possible. Specific details about the everyday lives, hopes, and dreams of the students with whom they are working help tutors build strong relationships. As trust is established through confidences that are explicitly valued by the tutors, tutors also gain more information to help plan effective lessons.

The Student Profile

Knowing a student means knowing about that person's strengths, interests, experiences, learning style preferences, multiple intelligences, and learning needs—all of which can be collected in a student profile early in the tutoring program and added to as more information is shared or demonstrated. This growing body of information can be used to plan each lesson.

Strengths, interests, experiences: During their tutor training session, tutors will complete an "All About Me" profile that is identical to the one they will complete with students during the initial tutoring session (see page 48). Students will identify information about their strengths, interests, and experiences at this time. Tutors will add to this list as more strengths, interests, and experiences emerge during tutoring sessions. These lists should be shared with the classroom teacher.

Learning style preferences: In his work on learning style preferences, Robert Sternberg taught us that the question is not "How smart are you?" but rather, "How are you smart?" In the past, there was an assumption that all people learn in the same way. Thus, when people had difficulty learning, it was assumed that they were not intelligent enough to learn. In recent decades, though, there have been profound new discoveries about how differently people learn. Also, research shows that matching learning style preference to teaching style results in higher achievement, greater interest in the subject, and greater enjoyment of learning.

Consider that many people who succeed in school are primarily visual learners, yet our research shows that the majority of students recommended for tutoring are kinesthetic learners. Tutors need to address students' learning style strengths.

This is not surprising, really. Good teachers have always taught in ways that address multiple learning style preferences—multiple pathways to learning. The students who are recommended for reading tutoring invariably do not learn in ways that the majority of the population learns. The key to tutoring success is to find the ways that individual students learn best and to use those approaches in tutoring—not teach according to the learning style preferences of the tutor or teacher.

There are many different approaches to learning style preferences. The one we advocate is simple and straightforward, involving ways the brain perceives and processes information, or *perceptual modality preference*. We focus on three different preferences: visual, kinesthetic, and auditory. Many people have a single most dominant preference while others have more than one. These preferences may also vary depending on the task at hand.

Tutors may use the information about types of learners to ask their students what they feel their learning style preferences are. They should also record in their observations things that they notice during tutoring that give insight into the learning style preferences of their students.

- **Visual learners** learn best through seeing things and writing things down to remember them. They have difficulty with verbal directions, often needing them to be repeated. They understand maps quite easily and remember details if they have mental pictures of them. Visual learners will be particularly sensitive to facial expression and body language. Tutoring that incorporates visual learning style preference will ensure that words are written down, that color is used to highlight or underline new words or parts of words, and that students have the opportunity to create graphic representations of what they have read, using mind maps or any of the graphic organizers mentioned in Chapter 7.
- **Kinesthetic learners** learn best when they can move while learning. They excel in learning from and through physical experience and they remember things well if they have had a chance to manipulate objects. People with a kinesthetic learning style preference get into trouble for touching things they are not supposed to or for taking things apart without directions for putting them back together. To the surprise of others, kinesthetic learners usually reassemble things perfectly through their "tinkering." Tutoring that incorporates kinesthetic learning style preference will ensure that students have frequent breaks to stretch, get a drink of water, and move about. Kinesthetic approaches include using word cards that students can pick up and put down, or prefix, suffix, and root word cards that students can assemble to make new words. (These are easily made from file cards or even by cutting an 8-1/2 by 11 piece of paper into smaller pieces.)
- **Auditory learners** learn best through listening without writing. They enjoy talking with others and need maps and charts explained to them orally. To learn best, they read aloud, discuss things with others, and report back orally. Our research shows that only a small percentage of students recommended for reading tutoring are auditory learners. Auditory tutoring approaches include having students read aloud and make up jingles to remember rules. These learners will thrive on repeated tape recordings of themselves reading aloud, listening to the differences in their reading over time.

Multiple intelligences: *Multiple intelligences* is a phrase coined by Howard Gardner in *Frames of Mind: The Theory of Multiple Intelligences.* Gardner initially identified seven types of intelligence, as follows:

- **Verbal/Linguistic:** People with verbal/linguistic intelligence excel at use of words. They focus on what is said (words) rather than how it is said (tone), focus on words rather than pictures or images, and enjoy word games.
- **Logical/Mathematical:** Those with logical/mathematical intelligence excel at numbers and logical sequence, think in wordless and imageless concepts, and enjoy finding logical flaws.
- **Spatial:** Students with spatial intelligence excel at visual images. They have a strong sense of direction, enjoy mazes and visual puzzles, and prefer reading texts with many illustrations or charts.

- **Bodily/Kinesthetic:** Many students selected for tutoring in reading have bodily/kinesthetic intelligence and excel in bodily awareness and physical skills, such as a sport or multiple sports. They often get their best ideas while physically active, perhaps while swimming or walking; they work well with their hands; and they cannot sit for long. In order to learn a new skill, they need to practise or do it.
- **Musical:** People with musical intelligence excel at singing or playing a musical instrument. With adolescents, this may mean that they are involved in a rock group outside of regular school hours. They remember best if learning is accompanied by music and are able to sing back or play a piece of music after hearing it once or twice.
- **Interpersonal:** Students with strong interpersonal intelligence excel at interacting with others. They enjoy being with others and learning through interaction with others. They often have numerous friends and are known as social individuals. Oftentimes, their friends come to them for advice.

Teachers should remind tutors to regularly update these profiles as more information is gained. "Student Profile Summary," available as a template in the Appendixes, is a tool for summarizing valuable information gathered over time. The classroom teacher or another tutor would benefit from having one about a tutored student.

Student Profile Summary

Name: _Jamal W._   Age: _13_   Grade: _9_

Strengths	- excels at sports, especially skateboarding and snowboarding - enjoys and does well in physical education, broad based technology subjects, and drama - working with his hands
Interests	- enjoys action films and comedies - enjoys outdoor activities - wants to learn how to read a manual for ATVs
Experiences	- enjoys working on outboard motors, ATVs, chain saws - works part time at his father's small engines shop - won first prize in local soap box derby
Learning Style/ Multiple Intelligences	- seems to have a strong preference for kinesthetic approaches to learning - finds learning from written text difficult - good physical skills; likes to be physically active - sitting still for any length of time is difficult
Learning Needs	- classroom teacher indicated that Jamal was reading 2 to 3 grades below grade - special education teacher reported that Jamal had been tested in Grade 6 and diagnosed as having a specific learning disability - has problems with decoding and comprehending written text - needs help with identifying phonemes in multi-syllable words - needs help with spelling and vocabulary
Suggestions	- have him keep a personal dictionary - use graphic organizers to aid comprehension - use prior knowledge of sports and technology to select appropriate reading texts - act out scenes from stories, use plays and skits as texts - use computer based approaches and resources - provide frequent breaks and changes in activities

- **Intrapersonal:** People with intrapersonal intelligence excel at individual reflection and have a realistic understanding of themselves. They think through difficult situations on their own, have special hobbies or interests that they keep mostly to themselves, and often are self-employed as adults.

Most people have combinations of the above intelligences. If tutors are aware of these intelligences, they will more readily understand and be able to use them to support student learning. For instance, if a student has strong musical intelligence, a tutor might encourage the student to bring music to the tutoring session or to have the student hear the rhythm of reading by over-emphasizing that rhythm in modelled reading. Students would also be encouraged to read aloud with the same kind of over-emphasis of rhythm.

The First Day of Tutoring

Establishing a positive rapport between tutor and student is highly important. On the first day of tutoring, teachers can provide tutors with information sheets, such as "All About Me," and either ask them to have students fill them in or, if students are unable to write well, have them engage students in discussion based on the sheet, offering information about themselves, too.

All About Me

Name: _Jeremy Beane_   Nickname (if I have one): _Beaner_

Age: _14_   School: _Clearis Secondary School_

Courses I am taking right now and teachers' names:

Course	Teacher
English	Ms. Fernandez
Math	can't remember
Learning Strategies	Mr. Kokatilo
Phys Ed	Mr. Nelson

Foods I like to eat _KD and pizza pops_

TV shows I like to watch _Monster Garage and Family Guy_

Songs, groups, or kinds of music I like _System of a Down_

Hobbies I have _dirt biking and working on cars_

Pets I have and their names: _Ruff, German Shepherd_

Sports I like to watch _Hockey_

Sports I like to play _dirt biking_

If I could have four people—dead or alive, real or fictional—to lunch with me, I would invite

my grandpa   _Stewie Griffin_

Janna (girlfriend)   _Matt (best friend)_

If I was stranded on a deserted island and could have just one piece of reading material with me, it would be

Auto Mechanics

If I could change one thing about myself, it would be _height - I want to be taller_

One thing I would never change about myself is _my friends_

Beyond that, one thing I'm good at is _dirt biking_

I think a good friend should always _be there for you_

Such an activity not only provides an opportunity for introduction, but also helps tutors gain insight into student attitudes towards reading and writing. By discussing student interests, tutors can identify potential subjects for later reading activities.

On the first day, it is a good idea for tutors to bring in a picture or item of personal significance—one that is appropriate for school—to share with their students and ask their students to bring in a picture or item of significance to the next meeting. This sharing shows tutors open to feeling vulnerable, just as students will need to be. It helps create a safe environment for tackling what is often one of the students' greatest challenges: reading.

Reading Interest and Attitude Survey

Another good way for tutors to get to know students is to engage them in discussion based on a "Reading Interest and Attitude Survey." The tutor could take notes during an informal talk with the student or, together, tutor and student could enter survey information on a computer. It is recommended that teachers direct tutors to "scribe" for students and draw out student responses: in a majority of cases, if they are trying to complete a form on their own, students are impeded from responding by an inability to write. As the example shows, the information gained about the student's past experiences with reading helps the tutor shape future planning. Once the form is complete, the tutor should share this information with the teacher at the next teacher–tutor meeting. A blank reproducible form appears on page 141.

Other activities can also take place during this initial meeting. The important thing is that it be as positive as possible.

Reading Interest and Attitude Survey

Name: _Frannie_   Date: _September 21, 2006_

Question	Student Response
What are some of your earliest memories about reading?	I remember Mrs. Burke reading to us on the carpet in Gr. 1.
Did your parents read to you? If they did, what are some stories you remember?	No. Don't remember
What do you remember about how you learned to read?	That it was hard. I was good at the alphabet
Did you have some favorite books when you were young? What do you remember about them?	Love You Forever — remember the teacher reading it to us
What makes reading a positive experience for you?	Something short and not boring
What makes reading difficult for you?	I get confused. I don't know some words.
What kinds of reading material do you find the most interesting? the least interesting?	Reading about celebrities and advice and stuff. Don't like school reading.
Do you sometimes have difficulty pronouncing words? If so, what do you do when you come to a difficult word?	Yes. Skip it.
Do you sometimes have difficulty understanding what you read? If so, what do you do when that happens?	Yes. Ask someone.
Have you ever worked with a tutor or someone who tried to help you before? What worked? What didn't?	Yes. She was nice to me and brought me Teen People.
What kinds of texts do you prefer to read? Newspapers? Magazines? Graphic novels? Novels? Stories? On what subjects?	Newspapers aren't so great. Teen magazines and real life stories are good. I like stuff on relationships and fashion.
What kinds of movies, television programs, and computer games do you like to watch or play?	Scary Movie 4, America's Top Model, The OC, no computer games
How can I help you with your reading? What would you like to work on?	Not sure. Just get better at it.

Creating an Effective Tutoring Plan

Effective tutoring plans are based on using students' strengths to address their learning needs. Using materials and activities that will engage the students is of critical importance, particularly with boys.

Classroom teachers and tutors will work together to establish and review the goals and strategies for each student being tutored. Based on these goals, as well as specific student interests, strengths, and needs, the tutor will create a tutoring plan for each session. The plan proposed in this manual is adaptable to many different contexts. It includes a number of components with descriptions of what to include in each one.

Plans are meant to serve as guides for tutors, not as exhaustive lists. Each session will vary according to student need, what has been learned previously, and the availability of resources. Not all of the components need to be part of each tutoring session, but the tutor should include all of them over every two to three sessions. An example of a completed tutoring plan follows on page 51.

Student Profile/Interest: The student's strengths, interests, and learning needs drive the creation of any tutoring plan. In the Student Profile section, the tutor writes down, in a phrase, one piece of information about the student that has a bearing on this lesson. Possible entries include *preference for reading sports magazines, kinesthetic learning style preference, able to predict,* or *learned 3 new sight words last time.*

Lesson Topic: In one or two phrases, the topic to be covered in the session is noted. For example, on the first day, the topic might be *Getting to know each other* or *Using a running record to diagnose student need.* As the tutor gets to know the student better, the topics will increasingly focus on areas of identified need, for example, *Learning how to use a fix-up strategy when confused* or *Learning how to use the index to find information.*

Learning Outcomes/Expectations: These are clear statements of what a student will know or be able to do as a result of explicit instruction. They provide the focus for planning, instruction, and assessment. Classroom teachers may supply tutors with learning outcomes/expectations based on provincial and state government curriculum documents related to literacy. There are also reading continuums that can be readily adapted to tutoring situations. Initially the outcomes/expectations are jointly created through teacher–tutor dialogue. As tutoring progresses, it becomes unnecessary for the tutor to discuss each tutoring plan beforehand with the classroom teacher.

Some examples of outcomes include the following:

- *The student will be able to identify the main idea and explain details that support the main idea.*
- *The student will be able to read aloud, demonstrating understanding of the material and awareness of audience.*

As tutors get to know their students, they will identify the skills already mastered, those that need reinforcement, and those that are new. To the greatest extent possible, students should help select outcomes. They will often have a good sense of what they need to work on, and

A tutoring plan for each meeting is essential.

Tutoring Plan

Student: _John_   Date: _Sept. 19_

Student Profile/Interest: _Visual learning style preference; snowboarding_

Lesson Topic	How to Read an Informational Text
Learning Outcomes/ Expectations	- identify main idea - explain how details support the main idea
Tutoring Session Goal	- John will be able to identify the main idea of the snowboarding article and select the five most important details that support that idea
Learning Materials	- magazine article on snowboarding - tape recorder - previously prepared taped reading of article by tutor
Before-Reading Activities	- have brief discussion of student's experiences with snowboards, skateboards, biking, etc. to activate prior knowledge - examine visuals that accompany the magazine article - invite student to make predictions about the main idea, supporting information, and author's purpose included in the article
During-Reading Activities	- play the first paragraph of the taped article - have John follow along in the text - invite John to confirm or revise predictions about main idea, related information, and author's purpose - continue to play audiotape or invite the student to read the next part out loud - during reading, stop from time to time to check for understanding and revise predictions accordingly
After-Reading Activities	- use a graphic organizer to plot out main idea, supporting details, and author's purpose - encourage John to support suggestions with evidence from the text
Strategies for Addressing Special Needs	- tape recording of the article - use of computer program for writing
Observations/ Feedback/ Assessment	- John listened well to tape recording, but after the first page got restless and wanted to read the rest out loud for himself - read the part about snowboarding techniques with enthusiasm - when asked to explain what the techniques meant, he was able to connect them to a personal experience with his dirt bike - got stuck on some of the more technical vocabulary - good progress on the graphic organizer—used Inspiration software
Reflections	- made a list of the words with which John had difficulty - will put them on flash cards and add them to John's personal dictionary - John really enjoyed reading about snowboarding, connected personally with the experiences of the author Next steps: - find an article on dirt biking for next time - reinforce main idea, supporting details, and author's purpose

tutors might end a session by asking students what they want to focus on in upcoming sessions. Tutors can support this process by giving options from which students can select. By being involved in planning, students assume more control over their learning, tutors improve their chances of engaging the students in learning, and the students are usually more motivated to improve their reading.

Tutoring Session Goal: In a short phrase, the tutoring goal being addressed in the session is identified. A quick check should show that the tutoring plan supports the successful achievement of the goal.

Learning Materials: It is important to keep track of the learning materials needed for each tutoring session. There are three types to consider:

- resources needed in order to implement the tutoring session (e.g., overheads, flip charts, markers, chart paper, pre-made flash cards, computer, LCD projector, equipment, graphic organizers)
- materials needed by the student (e.g., various writing materials, scissors, glue sticks, newspapers, magazines, chart paper, dice)
- text(s) to be used, with attention paid to the title, the kind of text (narrative, informational, graphic), the level of difficulty, and the connection with student interests/needs

Tutors should be reminded to check with the classroom teacher, the school librarian, and the special education teacher for materials that the school already has.

It is surprising just how quickly one can forget these details; recording them is important both to ensure that all materials are in readiness and to have a record for future reference. In addition, at the end of the tutoring program, these notes can be used to summarize which materials and texts were most effective: this information is useful for the student and the classroom teacher.

Before-Reading Activities: In this section, the activity that will be used before reading the text with the student is noted. Possible activities include getting to know the student, motivating the student, gaining diagnostic information, establishing personal connections with the text, establishing a purpose for reading, providing opportunities to learn new vocabulary, helping the student make predictions about the reading material, and activating prior knowledge about the topic. (See Chapter 6 for more detail on before-reading activities.)

During-Reading Activities: This section describes what will be done during the reading of the text. Some examples of during-reading activities include confirming predictions, using fix-up strategies, checking for understanding, and developing student awareness of effective reading strategies. (See Chapter 7 for more detail on during-reading activities.)

After-Reading Activities: This section describes what will be done after the reading of the text. Examples of after-reading activities include confirming predictions, checking for understanding, rereading for understanding, providing opportunities for personal response, and using information in the text for a new purpose. (See Chapter 8 for more detail on after-reading activities.)

Strategies for Addressing Special Needs: If the student has a special learning need as identified by the classroom teacher, this section is used to record any strategies that address those needs. A few examples: For visual memory skill needs, tutors might use books on audiotape; for needs in written language skills, tutors might use the *Word Cue* computer program; for building attention skills, they might offer a stress ball; and for needs in visual perception, they might use large-print books.

Observations/Feedback/Assessment: This section describes one way that the tutor will monitor student progress and states why that approach will be used. Here are some examples:

- Make observations about student strengths to use in a future lesson.
- Identify areas for instruction during next meeting.
- Provide informal feedback about aspects of reading such as decoding skills, comprehension, or the ability to make personal connections.
- Maintain a record of improvement, progress, and performance levels, noting dates.

Reflections: This section features the tutor's reflections on the student's behavior, attitude, and performance during the tutoring session. During face-to-face meetings with tutors, teachers can communicate questions to serve as a guide:

- To what degree did the student achieve today's goal?
- Was there any unexpected learning—a surprising achievement?
- What worked today and what didn't work?
- What are some suggestions for next time?
- What might be a more appropriate resource or strategy for this student?

The Importance of Tutor–Student Rapport

Strong rapport is the foundation of successful tutoring. Through getting to know students as *persons*, tutors build trust and learn information that supports effective tutoring plans. Oftentimes, tutors learn information about their students that is equally beneficial for teachers to know. In their face-to-face meetings, effective teachers ask tutors what they have learned that they might be able to follow up in the classroom.

Similarly, teachers will have news about students that is helpful and likely important for tutors to know. For instance, tutors can help celebrate school or extracurricular successes, giving further acknowledgment to students who often receive little recognition. There are other types of information, as well, that tutors need to have. They need to know of student illness or absence, of unfortunate events that have unfolded in the class or school, and of unfortunate events in the students' home lives. It is also helpful for them to be aware of any special events happening at the school. These types of information help tutors connect to students' lives—and to understand if student attention or achievement is not what is expected.

When tutors hear about student achievement or recognition in non-tutoring areas, they can celebrate with their students. "Ali! I hear that your group is going to play at the assembly next week! That's awesome!"

Chapter 5 Principles of Effective Tutoring

Tutoring is most effective when it improves the student's reading ability in terms of **decoding**, or getting the words right, and comprehending text. Many pre-teen and adolescent readers decode words fairly competently, but struggle to **comprehend**, to make meaning and see significance in what they read. Comprehension, though, is at the heart of reading. The goal of reading is to understand what has been read: readers can then ascertain what is important to them personally.

When dependent readers are asked what makes a good reader, they tend to say that a good reader "gets the words right" and "says them fast"—they ignore comprehension. It does not occur to them that when it comes to reading, meaning making is the key. Whereas pronouncing the words correctly and saying them at a good pace are apparent to any listener, comprehending the words is invisible. It is a misconception to believe that if readers are saying the words correctly and quickly, they are making sense of the text. These abilities do *not* necessarily go hand in hand.

Using Explicit, Strategic Instruction

Explicit instruction makes comprehension visible. With teacher guidance, tutors can model exactly what their brains are doing to make sense of what has been read. And yes, explicit instruction can be used to model decoding strategies, too. Strong readers have many strategies for getting the words right. (See Chapter 10 for word study ideas.)

Dependent readers need to gain a tangible understanding of what comprehension looks like. Through *explicit* instruction, tutors can help provide this. By sharing strategies in this book, teachers help tutors turn their own subconscious reading habits into explicit teaching. In the training session, through ongoing communication using a canvas bag or wire basket, and with periodic face-to-face meetings, teachers can share and remind tutors of various strategies. This support is particularly important in the initial month of tutoring: tutor–student dialogues within this book give tangible, helpful examples for tutors learning how to do this.

A closely related issue is that dependent readers do not monitor their comprehension. They do not use fix-up strategies when confused because they do not realize the need to be aware of themselves as readers. Rarely have they been taught metacognitive skills. **Metacognition** is thinking that is aware of itself as thinking—it refers to readers' abilities to think about themselves as readers and note how they use specific strategies to help their own comprehension.

Effective readers use strategies when they read on their own: they are independent, *strategic* readers who have multiple ways of thinking, or habits of mind, to get meaning from a text. For example, think about how fluent readers approach reading a newspaper and consider the strategies likely used:

- They glance at the article's title, which activates prior knowledge about the topic.
- They skim to get the gist of the text.
- They read what interests them, slowing down if they get confused, and rereading or reading on, and looking at visuals to aid comprehension.
- They may decide to chat about a piece of information from the article with friends, colleagues, or family members later on.

The goal of tutoring is to have students become this kind of reader, someone whose habits of mind support meaning making. In order to achieve this goal, the instruction must be both *explicit* and *strategic*. The supported direction of the classroom teacher is critically important, particularly in the early weeks of tutoring. As tutors gain experience, more and more they will be able to set strategic goals and make explicit reference to the particular strategies and cueing systems of successful readers—their *habits of mind*. Essentially, the goal of any tutor is to become unnecessary. Tutoring has succeeded when students can activate reading strategies independently and silently, and do this as a habit every time they read.

In addition to ensuring that instruction is explicit and strategic, teachers are wise to incorporate two principles in their tutoring programs:

- Start where each student is at and set appropriate goals.
- Monitor and assess student progress, sharing this with the student.

Starting Where the Student Is at and Setting Goals

Students will learn only when two conditions are met: that instruction builds on what they can already do and builds on what they are interested in.

Even before the tutor arrives, the classroom teacher will have conducted an assessment that indicates the reading level of all students to be tutored. Various types of assessment practices exist in all school boards: we encourage teachers to include personal observation in addition to measures required by their boards. Teacher observation often provides insightful information that is extremely useful for tutoring. Such assessments help diagnose areas of weakness so that instruction can be tailored to help learners improve their reading *where they are at the time*. It is on the basis of these assessments that the teacher will set initial tutoring goals.

Additional assessment should be conducted at the end of the tutoring program. If the program lasts for a full academic year, teachers might implement a mid-year assessment; however, regular classroom reading performance and teacher observation, as well as tutor observations recorded in the tutoring plans, continue to provide strong data on which to base tutoring goals and plans. Over the course of the tutoring and based on their tutoring observations, tutors may well suggest modification of the goals or addition of new goals: as always, the ongoing communication between tutor and teacher is critical to success.

Administering the "All About Me" activity and the "Reading Interest and Attitude Survey" will yield a wealth of knowledge about students that can be used to create tutoring plans (see templates in the Appendixes). We recommend that tutors administer these, for they provide initial "ice breakers" for tutors and students; they also enable tutors to share the information about themselves with students, providing a mechanism for building the relationship.

Information from simple diagnostic assessments is needed to show where learners are at in terms of reading skills. For the first session or two, tutors can work with students to complete diagnostic assessment forms provided by the teacher. They can ask students to read aloud texts of 200 to 300 words, preferably at the level the classroom teacher has determined that students can handle easily (the independent reading level). Tutors can make careful observations about comprehension based on responses to the questions that follow. If the reading material chosen proves to be too difficult—that is, the student makes 5 to 10 errors in the first half of the selection—then the tutor needs to pick something easier to read and continue the diagnostic assessment with that piece. Tutors should be advised to bring at least three texts at different reading levels to early tutoring sessions until they become familiar with students' reading abilities. A sample diagnostic reading assessment follows on pages 57 and 58.

The completed diagnostic reading assessment makes a useful handout for tutors. A template of the simple form is provided in the Appendixes.

Diagnostic Reading Assessment

Passage to be read by student:

Reality Bites

There are better things I could do on a Tuesday night, but somehow I find myself glued to the tube, entranced by a show named after a cosmic collapse. Supernova is a TV show supposedly looking for a lead singer to front a newly created rock band comprised of legends like Motley Crue's Tommy Lee, Metallica's Jason Newsted and Guns and Roses' Gilby Clarke. They aren't really looking for a lead singer — they are looking for money.

It's become cool to sell a product before you've even created it — and the product is a band that has yet to create an album. The crazy thing is, we are buying the product. People are paying money to phone in and choose their favorite for the "lead singer" position. We are also buying the product because we are watching the show. The higher the ratings, the more CBS can charge for commercial time. There have been many rock and pop bands created by the entertainment industry — the Backstreet Boys were notorious. They were infamous and heavily criticized for years. But the last decade has seen a rebirth of the rock band as a corporate creation. And it's got me wondering: how did rock music allow itself to be tamed?

Words: 210

Simple Diagnostic Reading Assessment

Student's Name: _Chris_   Date: _Sept. 19, 2006_

Title of Reading Passage: _Reality Bites   2 min 10 seconds aloud_

Make observations based on the following questions.

Decoding Questions: While reading, does the student

☑ Skip words?
Skipped "and" — not important

☐ Guess unknown words based only on the first letter or two?
_No_

☑ Substitute words that make sense in the sentence?
Said "could be doing" instead of "could do" (semantic and syntax OK)

☑ Substitute words that do not make sense, but fit with sentence syntax (structure)?
Said "cool" instead of "crazy" — didn't make sense but used initial grapheme

☑ Pause when reading aloud?   (never   sometimes   (often))

Comprehension Questions: During reading, does the student

☑ Notice when the words are not making sense?
Usually — self-corrected comic to cosmic

☐ Try a fix-up strategy? (Examples: slowing down, rereading, pausing and thinking)
just slowed down

☐ Make predictions about what will happen next?
_no_

☐ Ask questions and clarify ideas?
_no_

☐ Read with appropriate expression and phrasing that communicates sentence meaning?
Not much expression — missed the critical tone of the text

☐ Pay attention to punctuation? (Examples: pausing at periods, having the voice go up at the end of questions)
No: didn't pause at periods or commas and missed saying the last sentence as a question

Ask a few questions when the student is done reading and make notes.

Comprehension Questions: After reading, can the student

☐ Retell the main idea?   (His comment shows accurate, but simple understanding
It was about rock bands on TV —he didn't mention the criticism of non-existent rock band as product.)

☐ Provide relevant supporting details to the main idea? (His comment here is inaccurate. The text says,
There is a new album coming out   "have yet to create an album.")

☐ Make a personal connection to an idea in the text? (Some personal connection is evident; tutor could ask him to elaborate
I don't listen to that old stuff.   on this, for example: How does what you listen to differ from "that old stuff.")

☐ Describe a main character's actions (if the text is a narrative)?   (His comment here shows accurate
Tommy Lee, Jason Newsted and Gilby Clarke are in a band.   and simple understanding.)

☐ Explain the problem and the solution (if the text is a narrative)?   (His comment here is worrisome if he is
How did rock music allow itself to be tamed   unable to explain it and put it in his own words.)

With the initial administration of this assessment, the teacher will normally provide information about items in the Comprehension sections, such as the main idea and relevant details.

The teacher can provide the tutor with explicit feedback on answers (see teacher comments in the Comprehension sections) and aid the tutor in interpreting the diagnostic information and creating next steps. For example, with teacher support, a tutor's observations might be expanded to read as follows:

Chris is a Grade 10 student who seems to have strong grapho-phonemic awareness. He says the words on the page quite accurately (if slowly). Chris only made one semantic error, so he seems to be paying attention to meaning as he reads. However, his lack of interacting with the text, his trouble with fluency (pauses, phrasing, and intonation) and his limited answers suggest that, regardless of his few semantic errors, his comprehension may be a problem. He had trouble providing relevant supporting details and he didn't explain the concluding idea; he just read aloud parts of the final sentence. Chris needs to be encouraged to re-phrase ideas in his own words, and eventually, look for bias and tone in a text. He would benefit from before and during reading strategies where the tutor thinks aloud and explicitly models how he makes connections and understands what he reads. Chris's reading speed and fluency is also of concern as it seems to be too slow to support meaning making. The strategies in Chapter 10 of Tutoring Adolescent Readers, such as expressive reading, Readers Theatre, and taped oral readings, would be of particular benefit to him.

More focus questions are provided in reproducible format in Chapters 6, 7, and 8. Asking these will help identify with which reading skills the student is struggling. When the tutor diagnoses an area of weakness for the student, the tutor then knows exactly what to focus on in the next session—this becomes a tutoring goal.

One thing that tutors would do well to remember pertains to engaging their students. After the initial sessions, students benefit when they can become more directly involved in their own learning. Asking students to provide input into their learning increases their engagement. According to brain research, when human beings feel they have choice, they automatically pay stronger attention and feel more ownership for their learning.

Choice can be structured into the tutoring plans for each day. For example, at the start of a tutoring session, the student could be asked to choose between two selected texts: both texts might be articles on motocross at the student's independent reading level. At the end of a tutoring session, the student could consider a question like this: "In our next session, would you prefer to work on word attack strategies or how to get the main idea from a text?"

It is always important to find out what the student wants to know and use this to set the reading goals. For example, if the student is interested in getting a driver's licence, then an enterprising tutor could find the driver's handbook and drive testing sites on a government Web site and practise the skill of finding the most important, rather than the most interesting information.

In addition to applying informal diagnosis and student interests, tutors need to learn to rely on their own observations to create tutoring plans. One of the key skills that effective tutors have is "kid-watching," or making observations that will inform instruction. Teachers can support the development of this skill by looking at tutoring plan observations and

Remember, learners will not develop a skill after only one session. It will take several sessions and many different approaches to help them reach their goals and truly make a skill a habit of mind. For example, learning to pay attention to punctuation and understanding how it helps construct meaning will take many sessions of work.

letting tutors know which observations are particularly well done. In addition, the student profile and tutoring plan (outlined in Chapter 4) will both contain precise information from which each successive tutoring plan can be created. For example:

Notes from Observations and Reflections Last Session	Ideas for Next Session
-Terina seems unable to notice when she is confused when reading, but she really enjoyed looking at the Teen Celebrity magazine.	-Work on "noticing when we are confused" by asking questions as we read (habit of strong readers). I'll model and Terina can practise on Teen Celebrity article.

A beautiful thing about teaching and learning is that it is cyclical: once tutors understand where their students are at and goals are set, monitoring and assessing student progress will enable new goal setting and development of further strategic, explicit instruction.

The Importance of Monitoring and Assessing Student Progress

To monitor and assess student growth in reading, tutors need to provide specific and explicit feedback, and to keep records that demonstrate growth. This aspect of tutoring provides the starting point for most tutor–teacher communication—whether that is through brief written notes or face-to-face meetings. Teachers will also use tutor information to inform their own planning to meet students' individual needs. When tutors understand this, they come to realize the importance of their observations and record keeping and invariably take more care in these matters. It is good to highlight the importance of this information in the tutor training session as well as to reinforce it through ongoing communication.

Providing Specific and Explicit Feedback

In order to be successful, learners need to know what they are doing well and what they need to do differently. By paying careful attention to exactly what students do while reading, tutors can monitor their growth and provide positive, specific feedback. To be useful to students—and teachers—tutor feedback must be explicit, systematic, and corrective (Ysseldyke and Christensen 2002).

Teachers might provide tutors with the following helpful summary, "How to Provide Useful Feedback."

How to Provide Useful Feedback

When working with students, try to make feedback as useful, explicit, and systematic as possible.

- **Reinforce specific processes and strategies that students use successfully.**
  Example: *I noticed that when you came to that word "segregation" you realized you needed to pronounce it like "integration" because they have the same endings and then you wondered if there might be a connection between those two words.* (Instructional comment)

- **Explain what students need to do next to continue their progress.**
  Example: *When you read an information text, keep trying to make that distinction: what is* important *versus what is* interesting. (Instructional comment)

- **Give instructional feedback that relates directly to students' responses.**
  Example: *You made the prediction that Susanna must be the criminal because she was at the crime scene at the right time and had a motive based on your ability to infer.* (Instructional comment)

- **Praise both students' instructional and non-instructional behaviors.**
  Example: *You are really paying attention to punctuation when you read aloud and sound like you are asking a question here.* (Instructional comment) *Your perseverance will get you far. It's great that you keep trying.* (Non-instructional comment)

- **Model how to use a reading strategy.**
  Example: *When I start reading a graph, I look first at the title and try to figure out what the graph will show me. For instance, I think this graph will show me how the amount of junk food consumed by North Americans has been growing since the 1970s because the titles on each of the axes indicate junk food and the dates, beginning with 1970.*

- **Show the positive change from past to present performance.**
  Example: *Let's look at the first sequence map you completed in September and the one you've just done. In this first one, you included many details, some of which were really important and others that were not. In the one you've just completed, there are fewer details and all of them are important. Your identification of important detail is much stronger now.* (Instructional comment) *You are making great progress. Good for you!* (Non-instructional comment)

Keeping Records That Demonstrate Growth

The truism nothing succeeds like success applies well to reading. For dependent readers, improving their reading is hard work and they need to see evidence that their efforts are paying off. Tutors can be guided in how to demonstrate students' improvement to them. Ways of demonstrating growth include

- conducting self-assessment interviews with learners
- maintaining literacy portfolios, which are collections of student work
- writing final summary letters or more informal "good-bye" letters when the tutoring comes to an end

Self-Assessment Interviews

These interviews allow tutors and students to talk about growth and together conduct a student self-assessment. This type of self-reflection helps students see the value in the tutoring and reinforces the importance of attending tutoring sessions. The self-assessment interview can take the form of a list, such as the following, with the tutor assisting when the student cannot remember all of the things that he or she knows or uses. Note that the questions are from the student's perspective.

- How many different types of reading have I done?
- What is one new before, during, and after reading strategy I now use?
- When I come to a word I don't know, what strategies do I now use?
- How do I know my reading is getting better?

Teachers may ask tutors to use this self-assessment—or a variation of it—about every month to enable students to see growth.

Literacy Portfolios

Literacy portfolios are easy to build if tutors are just reminded to gather and date any kinds of records or written responses that students create during the tutoring sessions. Tutors and students alike will be surprised at how quickly samples accumulate and teachers can remind tutors to use these items to help students see their progress over time.

Students, as well as teachers and parents, appreciate the creation of literacy portfolios and benefit from the gathering of tutor and personal observations and insights. A literacy portfolio of student work might feature the following.

Sample responses to reading selections: During tutoring sessions, students complete a variety of reading activities, both in writing and orally. For example, students may make full sentences, mind maps or webs, charts, and sketches, and talk while tutors scribe their ideas. It is important for tutors to date these activities and ensure that they represent a range of responses to different kinds of texts—narrative, informational, and graphic texts—and demonstrate different levels of understanding and personal connection. Another idea is to include samples of short pieces read successfully, especially if the texts are written at increasing levels of difficulty.

Tables: Tables are an easy way to keep and provide evidence of what students have accomplished and still need to learn. Some sample tables for the literacy portfolio are shown below. Teachers should advise tutors to set up a similar table at the beginning of the tutoring sessions. Entry of information then becomes a tangible reinforcement of progress.

A number of different tables follow. Tutors will usually want to choose just one of these, depending on tutoring goals and duration of the tutoring program. Teachers should determine the kind of information that will be most useful to them, given their other tracking mechanisms, and have tutors complete tables that will complement or balance other information that is already being collected as a regular part of classroom monitoring.

This table provides a quick overview of what the student prefers to read and strategies the student is using.

Type of text and strategies used table

Date	Title of Text	Type of Text (Story, biography, article, photo essay, etc.)	Reading Strategy Used
Nov. 18	"Instructions" by Gaiman from *Wolf at the Door*	Fairy tale/poem	Rereading and think aloud

This table encourages student self-awareness and metacognition.

Awareness of reading strategies table

I use this reading strategy	Never	Sometimes	Often	Always
1. Rereading		✓ Sept. 29th		

These tables allow students to see progress in time spent reading, writing, and talking about what they have read. Teachers would naturally ensure that tutors understand the terms *independent* and *instructional*. For the second table, a tutor could work with a student to count the number of words in the passage.

Progress tables

Session Date	Time Spent Reading	Time Spent Talking	Time Spent Writing
Sept. 25	20 minutes	15 minutes	10 minutes

Session Date	Independent (Easy) Level Text	Total Number of Words	Instructional Level Text	Total Number of Words
Sept. 30	"Rabbit" by Graves from *Baseball, Snakes and Summer Squash*	88 words	"Summer Squash" by Graves from *Baseball, Snakes and Summer Squash*	200 words

Artifacts: These are visual and audio-visual materials that show concrete evidence of work in progress and work completed. Examples are photographs, audiotapes or videotapes of the tutor and learner working together, dated audiotapes of the student reading, and visual displays of student work. Given the technological resources and time involved in creating some of these artifacts, there needs to be clear communication between teachers and tutors on the need for them, provision of equipment by the teachers, and specific time frames of when tutors should collect and produce them.

Final Summation and "Good-bye" Letters

When tutoring programs come to an end, students will benefit if tutors prepare final summation letters. These letters are *not* formal assessments of student reading ability. They are a way for tutors to share their observations and insights with teachers, students, and their parents. Ideally, tutors and students would write much of these reports together. "Prompts to Writing a Final Summation Letter" could be used to guide thinking.

Prompts to Writing a Final Summation Letter

The final summation letter is an expectation of this tutoring program. It summarizes what the tutor has learned that may be used by the teacher or future tutors; it also gives closure for the student. This letter is written by the tutor and, if possible, with student input. It should be dated.

As with all communication that goes to students' homes, a draft of this letter is given to the classroom teacher who will read it carefully, noting any changes that need to be made. The final version should be put on school letterhead and given to the teacher. A copy will be made for school records and the original, signed by the tutor, will be sent to the student's home.

Student Learning Style and Strengths
- Identify the student's learning style preferences and multiple intelligences. Example: *Eyal is a kinesthetic learner who has strong interpersonal skills and who remembers things particularly well that he has learned through hands-on experience.*
- Consider what reading activities seemed most helpful in improving reading.
- Identify the reading strategies and skills the student demonstrated.

Student Likes and Interests
- Review the type of reading material that appeals to the student.
- Consider how areas of special interest were used to support reading development.

Student Attitudes
- Consider how the student felt about reading at the start of tutoring and also at the end of tutoring.
- Assess how the student feels towards tutoring.
- Assess the student's cooperation during tutoring sessions.
- Identify student contributions to the learning.

Student Areas of Need
- Identify specific before, during, or after reading skills that need further attention.
- Suggest additional kinds of reading experiences.

Student Progress
- Note changes or improvements in reading skills.
- Note changes or improvements in attitude towards reading.

Recommended Strategies and Approaches
- Please identify tutoring activities and strategies that you would recommend for next steps at home, school, or work.

Instead of preparing final summation letters, tutors might write more informal "good-bye" letters to the students they have worked with. During their time together, tutors and students probably developed good working relationships that may even have grown into friendship. In brief notes, tutors might convey their thoughts and feelings about the time spent working together. They could remind learners of some of the activities done together, some of the books read together, things that students can now do well, and gains made. They might praise students for their hard work and encourage them to keep reading.

If teachers or tutor coordinators know that tutors are undertaking to write either type of letter, they must see and review the drafts. Doing so will ensure that tutors do not overstate gains or inadvertently make inappropriate comments. For instance, a tutor might see great gains by the student, but not realize that the student has yet to meet grade-level expectations for reading. If the tutor writes, "BJ has made wonderful progress and is reading well both orally and silently," parents could easily interpret this to mean that BJ is now meeting grade-level expectations—his progress might have been strong, but he is still reading significantly below expectations. Once tutors have received teacher feedback, they can finalize their letters and pass them on. What follows is a model letter addressed to the student's parent.

December 11, 2006

Dear Ms. Seto:

I have enjoyed working with Keiko as her literacy tutor very much. Over the past few months, we have been doing many activities in our tutoring sessions. Below are some things that we have done during this time.

Keiko has many strengths: she is an auditory learner who comprehends texts better when she reads out loud and she understands instructions well when they are given orally. She is also an intrapersonal learner who enjoys thinking about what she reads and figuring out her beliefs and values in relation to an article. Keiko also has strong interpersonal skills and enjoys talking with me about what we are reading.

In terms of what we have read, Keiko really enjoys her CSI novels, as well as Internet and magazine articles on fitness and soccer. She is a big fan of CSI and her favorite activity is when she gets to read a section of the novel and explain it to me in her own words. She loves to comment on the characters' personalities on the show and in the novel. I think she finds reading these books easier because she already knows the characters. A writing activity that Keiko enjoys is creating newspaper articles based on "the latest development in the crime."

Keiko has a very positive attitude. She was rarely absent, always motivated and worked diligently in our sessions together. When encouraged, she would give feedback about what was working for her and what she would like to do the next time we got together.

Keiko has shown a lot of progress over the course of the tutoring. She is more willing to take chances in her reading and explanations. Even when she is unsure of herself, she tries to answer questions that I ask and, most important, she is beginning to get comfortable asking questions herself when she is confused. She is getting better at using fix-up strategies, like rereading, to make sure she understands what has been read. Keiko uses think aloud strategies very well and has become comfortable talking things out to help her comprehend as she reads.

Keiko continues to struggle with making inferences when reading—she has difficulty reading "between the lines." Keiko needs to continue to practise asking herself questions and making connections as she reads to monitor and increase her own understanding. Keiko has opinions about what is happening in the text, but sometimes has difficulty supporting her opinions with information from the text. She has found that creating graphic organizers, like mind maps, enable her to identify details that support her opinions and ideas.

Your support at home, including setting aside a quiet place for homework completion, makes a great difference. Your encouragement and support mean more than you may realize in helping Keiko find energy for what can be very hard work. Keiko should also be encouraged to keep reading crime and mystery novels. You might consider taking her to your local public library's mystery section and encouraging her to read other mystery writers.

I have had a great time working with Keiko. If you have any questions, please do not hesitate to contact the school.

Yours sincerely,

Dirk Doucette
Tutor

Chapter 6 Helping Students Before They Read

Pre-reading activities help readers to

- access prior knowledge
- interact with the text before reading
- make inferences
- draw comparisons
- make predictions
- identify difficult words
- construct meaning

Based on Beers (2003)

Even before they read the first sentence in a book, independent readers do a lot to prepare themselves for reading. They look at the front cover to get clues from the title, author, and pictures as to what the book is about. They check the back cover for a brief outline of the story or a summary of information contained in the text. They scan the author biography to learn about the author's background, interests, and other books. They consult the publisher blurbs to find out what other readers have found interesting about the book and why they recommend it. They look through the table of contents, if there is one, to gain an outline of the content. Independent readers are constantly thinking and asking themselves questions. *Will I like this book? Does it remind me of something I have read before? Is it going to be interesting or helpful to me? Will I be able to understand it? Will it tell me what I need to know?*

Dependent readers, on the other hand, do very few of these things. They often rush right in and start reading—they don't take time to ask themselves questions about the text. As a result, they are not mentally prepared to get meaning from the text. They have not given their brains enough time to get ready to read successfully.

Although successful readers may not always be conscious of the thought processes they use before reading, these processes play a critical role in preparing them to read. One of the most important factors in supporting learners in becoming independent readers is the ability to connect new information in a text with information they already know. That is how they make sense of what is on the page.

Setting Goals for Pre-reading Activities

Tutors can make it easier for learners to prepare for reading in many ways. For example, they could begin with an informal discussion about the content of the passage. This kind of informal talk not only focuses the learners' attention, but also prompts them to think about what they already know of the text content. *Activating prior knowledge*, as it is called, is one of the most important goals of pre-reading activities. It helps set a purpose for reading so that before readers begin to read a text, they will be primed to look for specific information. During the preliminary discussions, effective tutors encourage learners to express their thoughts or feelings about what they are going to read. This encouragement stimulates engagement with the text; it also helps learners make personal connections with the content, another important goal of pre-reading activities.

Pre-reading activities may also serve to help learners make predictions on what they are about to read. If it is a story, learners could predict what is going to happen. If it is a non-fiction text, they could anticipate what the author will tell them about the topic. By helping learners make predictions, tutors not only prepare them for reading, but also model what independent readers do to anticipate textual meaning. Teachers can support tutors in these kinds of activities by introducing them to strategies such as the anticipation guide and Probable Passage guide, both described later.

Tutors may also use pre-reading activities to help learners practise reading skills, such as sequencing information, finding cause-and-effect relationships, drawing comparisons, making inferences, and learning new vocabulary. "Focus Questions to Ask Before Reading," on page 70, gives a selection from which tutors can choose. Tutors should be reminded that for each tutoring session, they will generally choose only one pre-reading goal, such as drawing comparisons.

A number of specific reading strategies help learners achieve the goals of pre-reading. Below, several pre-reading strategies that have proven to be particularly effective in helping students get ready to read are explained. These strategies include focus questions; the K-W-L question strategy; content analysis; graphic organizers, such as semantic maps, thought webs, and pyramid outlines; anticipation guides; and Probable Passage. In each case, they have been adapted to a tutoring situation. Tutors need to be reminded to be realistic in their planning of strategy use, allocating anywhere from 5 to 15 minutes, depending on the familiarity of the topic and the difficulty of the text. As students often spend several tutoring sessions on the same text, these activities are well worth the time they take.

Focus Questions with Pre-reading Goals

Questions that focus on specific goals provide a simple, but extremely effective means of improving reading and thinking skills (Stauffer 1975). In a tutoring situation, discussing a few questions helps prepare the learner for reading a new text.

The chart on page 70 provides some sample questions, links the questions to specific pre-reading goals, and shows how they can be adapted to narrative and informational texts. Tutors would benefit from having a copy to remind them of pre-reading goals and questions to help achieve them.

If a tutor is using any before-reading strategies for the first time, the classroom teacher may want to prepare a worksheet or graphic organizer that the tutor can use with the student. The models provided in this chapter can be adapted to the text that the teacher wants the tutor to use. The teacher may also want to set a pre-reading goal for the session and show the tutor how to achieve that goal using the strategy recommended.

Learners are best served when they are asked a few focused questions instead of a barrage of diverse questions: the goal is for learners to pick up this habit of mind and come to ask questions on their own before beginning to read.

Focus Questions to Ask Before Reading

Pre-reading Goal	Sample Questions for Narrative Texts	Sample Questions for Informational Texts
Access prior knowledge	What story does the cover tell? Have you read another story of the same kind? What was it about?	What do you already know about this topic? How did you learn it? Does the topic of this text remind you of something you have previously heard or seen?
Interact with the text before reading	Does this story remind you of something you have previously seen or heard? Do the words and pictures on the cover make you want to read this book? If so, how?	What subject does the picture or illustration on the cover or in the text make you think about? What do you expect the author to explain or tell you about?
Make inferences	What do you think will be the main idea of this story? What do you think will be the main challenge faced by the characters?	What do you think will be the main topic of this text? Do you think you will find this text interesting? Explain why.
Draw comparisons	In what ways does the main character remind you of someone you have met or heard about? In what ways do you think this story will be similar to or different from other stories you have read or heard about?	What do you hope the author will tell you that you don't already know? In what ways do you think this information will be similar to or different from your own experience with this subject?
Make predictions	What do the pictures or illustrations on the cover suggest about the content of this book? From the information on the back and front covers, what can you tell about the main characters in the book?	What does the table of contents suggest that the author is going to explain about the topic? When you look at the title, what words do you predict will be used in this book?
Identify difficult words	On the first page, are there any words that are new to you? Can you guess the meaning of new words on the front or back cover?	In the table of contents or subheads in the text, are there any words that are new to you? As you skim, can you guess the meaning of one word that is new to you?
Construct meaning	What does the title tell you about the story? What do you think the characters in this story will learn about themselves and about others?	How do the pictures and words on the cover work together to make meaning? How might you use the information in this book?

K-W-L Question Strategy

In terms of developing lifelong reading skills, the most powerful questions are often not those that tutors or teachers create; rather, they are the questions that learners generate before they begin to read. Tutors need to know this.

Effective tutors model how to ask questions before reading, based on interest, wonderings, personal connections, or confusion. Beyond that, with teacher support, they may adopt a slightly more complex strategy for teaching dependent readers how to ask questions: K-W-L, or **Know-Wonder-Learn**.

Teachers may introduce tutors to K-W-L, a strategy first developed by Donna Ogle to help dependent readers both before and after they read a selection (Beers 2003). As a pre-reading strategy, K-W-L encourages learners to consider what they already know about the topic in the text they are about to read and what they hope to learn from the text. It also actively engages learners in determining what the information contained in the passage means to them personally, thus encouraging the creation of meaning. Furthermore, by asking learners to identify what they hope to learn from their reading, tutors encourage learners to make predictions, a key strategy used by independent readers. As a post-reading strategy, K-W-L serves as an excellent means of checking for understanding.

The tutor will need an example of K-W-L from the classroom teacher: this could easily be left in the canvas communication bag, with a note from the teacher such as, "When you are working on the development of the West assignment for history, you might use the enclosed K-W-L chart to help Nick identify what he already knows before he begins reading the text. Then, go back to the chart after he has finished the reading."

K-W-L can be readily adapted to tutoring situations by following these steps:

1. The tutor creates a chart either on paper or on the computer screen with three columns:

K (What I Know)	W (What I Want/Think I Will Learn)	L (What I Learned)

Students may lack background knowledge on the topic. The K-W-L chart or even simple questioning such as, "What do you know about the development of the West?" gives a strong indication of student familiarity with the content and concepts they are about to encounter. If student background knowledge is scant, tutors would be wise to generate it by turning to another pre-reading strategy, such as focus questions or a graphic organizer.

2. The tutor briefly introduces the main topic of the reading selection and asks the learner to share prior knowledge about the subject.

3. As the learner makes suggestions, the tutor writes them down under the first heading on the chart.

4. The tutor then uses the list generated by the student as the basis for a discussion on the topic. The discussion should flow naturally from what the learner already knows to what the learner does not know about the topic, but would like to learn.

Some learners prefer to work on the computer. If the school has computer software such as *Kidspiration*, *Inspiration* or *Smart Ideas*, it would be worthwhile to make it available to tutors for use in tutoring sessions.

5. The tutor writes the items identified by the student as "I want to learn" in the form of questions in the second column.

6. As a post-reading activity, the tutor and the learner together put the answers to the questions from column two in column three; however, if some questions remain unanswered, the tutor and the learner

could brainstorm for ideas about where they might obtain answers and use the identified sources in a subsequent tutoring session.

Content Analysis: Distinguishing Most Important Ideas

One effective way for tutors to prepare for a tutoring session is to conduct an analysis of the content of the passage they are about to use and make that information the basis for a pre-reading activity. This analysis is more realistic for tutors to do when they are working with a longer text that will be used over several tutoring sessions, perhaps a passage from a textbook. It would be helpful for tutors if classroom teachers identify and communicate the ideas they would like most stressed. A **content analysis** focuses on key concepts, facts, and generalizations in a passage and helps readers get ready to understand an informational text by introducing them to the main ideas contained in it. During the content analysis, the ideas in a text are arranged in a framework that shows how the key facts, concepts, and generalizations are related.

Research has proven that the technique is an effective process for establishing instructional objectives in the content areas (Cooter and Reutzal 1994). For tutoring purposes, a content analysis not only helps set goals for reading, it also provides learners with critical information that will help them understand what they are about to read.

The information in a text is analysed at three different levels of specificity:

- *facts*, or the individual bits of information or details provided by the author;
- *concepts*, or the categories used to organize or group the facts; and
- *generalizations*, that is, statements that summarize what the passage is about.

Following is a content analysis of an article on waste management.

Topic:	Article on Waste Management			
Generalization:	*This article explores the advantages and disadvantages of different methods of waste disposal.*			
Key Concepts:	Composting	Recycling	Incineration	Landfill
Main Facts: (Advantages)	reduces garbage	benefits environment	produces energy	can be used to reclaim land
	good fertilizer	creates jobs	requires less land	low cost
(Disadvantages)	high cost	requires sorting	air pollution	devaluation of property
	finding markets	high participation needed	cost	odour

How to Use Content Analysis as a Pre-reading Activity

Ideally, the teacher would prepare an outline or chart that sets out the key generalizations, concepts, and facts in the text and give it to the tutor. Before reading begins, the tutor would use the chart to engage the student in a discussion about the topic. The purpose is to determine what the student already knows about the topic and to anticipate and clarify some of the information dealt with in the article.

The teacher takes a few minutes to go over this framework with the tutor. The process prepares students for what they are about to read by focusing on what is important in the text. New content may present a challenge for all readers, but is especially problematic for those students who bring little background information to a new topic. They find it difficult to distinguish important ideas from those that are less important. A content analysis provides an excellent grounding in the information conveyed in the text and serves as a guide to that information. It also helps students fill in any gaps of knowledge as well as to analyse and organize critical details.

Below is a sample content analysis chart for a selection on recycling paper:

Facts (types of paper)	Concepts	Generalizations
• container board • boxboard • construction paper • paper pellets	• Why we should recycle paper • How to use recycled paper	• Recycling one ton of newspaper saves 19 trees.

A content analysis can also be used to preview a story such as *Romeo and Juliet*:

Events	Main Characters	Theme
• Boy meets girl. • Boy falls in love with girl. • Girl's and boy's parents are in a feud and would disapprove if they knew the boy and girl were in love. • Boy and girl seek help from a friendly friar. • Friendly friar gives girl potion that puts her in a deep sleep. • Boy thinks girl is dead and kills himself. • Girl wakes up to find boy is dead. • Girl kills herself.	Boy Girl Parents of girl Parents of boy Friendly friar	Parents' feud can have tragic consequences.

Some parts of the outline, for example, Advantages and Disadvantages of each of the waste disposal methods, could be left blank and filled in during or after the tutoring session.

Semantic Maps, Thought Webs, and Pyramid Outlines

Our research has shown that use of a computer to generate graphic organizers increases student engagement. Simple word-processing programs allow for students to draw shapes, insert text, and draw lines between them. Other programs, such as *Kidspiration*, *Inspiration* or *Smart Ideas*, are even easier to use and more powerful in going from a graphic organizer to a report or essay. If possible, enable students to work with these programs.

Teachers are wise to ensure that tutors are aware of the semantic map as an effective technique for introducing key vocabulary found in a new text. This knowledge could easily be communicated through the bag or wire basket mechanism.

Graphic organizers are visual ways of organizing and presenting information. In the context of pre-reading activities, they focus learner attention on what they are about to read and help them express and clarify their thoughts about the topic or story before reading it. Graphic organizers can help achieve many pre-reading goals. Selected organizers, including semantic maps, are explained below.

Use a Semantic Map to Pre-teach Vocabulary

Dependent readers benefit from being pre-taught vocabulary. Unlike independent readers who have many words at their disposal, most dependent readers have smaller reading than speaking vocabularies. This problem is compounded because they have difficulty making connections between the words they know and the words they don't. When independent readers come to a word they don't understand, they are often able to determine its meaning from context. Through tutoring, dependent readers can come closer to bridging that gap. When classroom teachers are supplying the text, it is helpful to tutors if teachers identify vocabulary they think may be problematic for students.

Tutors can help simply by providing learners with definitions of words that they anticipate will cause problems. They can model how to find the meaning of a word by using whatever dictionary is available at the school. They need to be reminded, however, that students, especially dependent readers, will have problems trying to remember a list of unrelated definitions.

A more effective technique for introducing vocabulary in a new text is the semantic map (Collins Block 1997). A **semantic map** helps readers visualize the relationships among words. It consists of a simple line diagram with the main idea written in the middle of the page with supporting words and concepts arranged in patterns around it. Each cluster of words is connected in some significant way to the main idea. Pre-teaching potentially challenging vocabulary by creating a map helps learners add words to their vocabularies by seeing the connections among words in a passage. As always, an example from the teacher for the tutors is helpful.

1. The tutor writes the key word, which represents the key concept in the passage, in the middle of the page (e.g., Blue Jeans).

2. The tutor then explains to the learner that the article explores several different aspects of blue jeans: their origin and history, the process used to manufacture them, and their contemporary cultural significance. The tutor writes these subtopics on the page and draws a line from each of them to the words "Blue Jeans" in the centre of the page.

3. The tutor discusses each of these concepts with the learner to make sure that they are understood.

4. Next, the tutor tells the student that in each section, the writer uses some words that might be new to the learner and before reading the passage together, they will go over each of them together.

5. The tutor then writes the words one at a time under each of the sub-headings and asks the learner to define them. If the student is unable to do so, the tutor adds the definition to the semantic map.

Use a Thought Web to Stimulate Prior Knowledge

Another way to help learners make connections between what they already know and what is contained in the text is through the use of a thought web. A **thought web** is a graphic organizer that encourages brainstorming. Although similar to a mind map, the prior-knowledge thought web will generate student knowledge that may or may not be part of the text that will be read. Once the student's prior-knowledge thought web is complete, the tutor might say: "You know a lot about this already! Let's see if any of this information is in the text—and if there is any new information that we learn."

1. The tutor begins by placing a key word, for example, the main topic or theme of the selection, in the middle of a large piece of paper. The tutor then asks the learner to state what he or she already knows about the topic or theme. Depending on the student's energy and engagement at the time, either the student or the tutor may do the writing. Some computer programs support this activity well. Again, the student or the tutor may control the computer, or the activity may be shared. The idea is to keep momentum in this brainstorming.

2. As the learner offers perceptions, the tutor asks for connections among them. The connections can be shown through lines drawn between various items. As the learner makes more suggestions, patterns and commonalities will gradually emerge.

3. The tutor encourages the learner to cluster the suggestions. As new suggestions are made, the tutor asks the learner to place them under the appropriate headings.

Use a Pyramid Outline to Focus Reading

A **pyramid outline**, written in the shape of a triangle, is a hierarchical graphic depiction of information contained in a text. The topics dealt with in the text are written in descending order from the top of the triangle to the bottom beginning with the main topic. Such hierarchies are effective tools used by teachers to present new knowledge to their students (Reutzal and Cooter 1994). They can easily be adapted to tutoring situations.

The triangle outline is completed by the tutor and the learner in the following sequence of steps. Teachers might want to photocopy "Semantic Maps, Thought Webs, and Pyramid Outlines: What They Look Like," so tutors have an example from which to work.

1. Before the tutoring session, the tutor writes the main topic of the selection on top of the triangle. The tutor then identifies the main subtopics and writes them below the main topic.

Semantic Maps, Thought Webs, and Pyramid Outlines: What They Look Like

Example of a Semantic Map

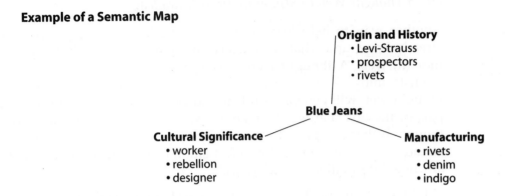

Origin and History
• Levi-Strauss
• prospectors
• rivets

Blue Jeans

Cultural Significance
• worker
• rebellion
• designer

Manufacturing
• rivets
• denim
• indigo

Example of a Thought Web

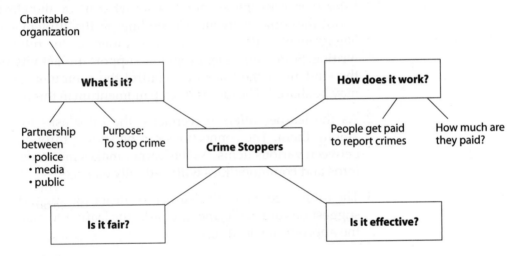

Charitable organization

What is it?

How does it work?

Partnership between
• police
• media
• public

Purpose: To stop crime

Crime Stoppers

People get paid to report crimes

How much are they paid?

Is it fair?

Is it effective?

Example of a Pyramid Outline

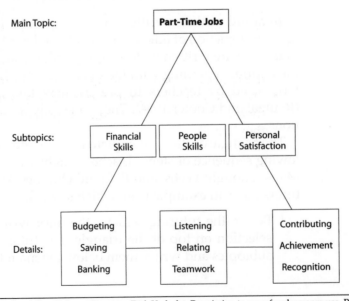

Main Topic: **Part-Time Jobs**

Subtopics: Financial Skills | People Skills | Personal Satisfaction

Details:
Budgeting / Saving / Banking
Listening / Relating / Teamwork
Contributing / Achievement / Recognition

2. In the tutoring session, the tutor uses the outline to introduce the selection and explain how the writer has organized it.

3. The tutor then invites the learner to watch for details that fit under each subtopic.

4. As they read the piece together, the tutor helps the learner fill in the details below each of the subtopics. As above, student motivation and energy guide the degree to which the tutor is involved in scribing or entering ideas. Sharing the task is fine.

Tutors can also use completed triangles as post-reading activities to check how well students comprehended the text and to clarify information.

Anticipation Guides

An **anticipation guide** is aptly named. It encourages learners to anticipate the text that is about to be read by focusing on some of the key ideas explored within it. It helps dependent readers apply a fundamental life skill: the need to anticipate the ideas that will be found in a text (Fisher and Frey 2004). An anticipation guide aims to develop interest in the upcoming text by pulling out main ideas, thereby building anticipation in the learner.

This strategy requires the tutor to determine a few key ideas in a text. If the text is selected by the teacher, it is helpful for the teacher to supply the ideas. If the text is provided by the tutor, the tutor would benefit from receiving "Introducing Anticipation Guides," on page 78, and seeing an example of an anticipation guide.

An anticipation guide can be used to achieve several pre-reading goals.

Anticipation guides help learners respond to a story or an information selection *after*, as well as before, reading. After reading, the tutor and the student can return to the anticipation guide and complete the after-reading checklist. They thereby gain excellent material for tutor–student discussion about the text.

- When students are invited to think seriously about the ideas in an article or story before they read, tutors can determine how much they know about the topic and how much preparation is needed to help them understand the text.
- When students are asked to take positions on issues raised in text, they gain an opportunity to engage with these issues in a low-risk environment.
- Creating an element of controversy motivates students to read the selection. For example, for an article about animal cloning, tutors may ask students if they would want to have a pet cloned. Tutors would take the opposite point of view from the students, articulating the benefits or advantages of their point of view.
- Students are better prepared to construct meaning when they and their tutors discuss the issues dealt with in the text even before they read.

Introducing Anticipation Guides

Anticipation guides are useful in teaching both fiction and non-fiction. The steps outlined below explain how to use these pre-reading tools in a tutoring context:

1. To prepare for a tutoring session, create three to five statements linked to ideas in the text that is to be read (see the example on cloning below).
   - Make sure that the statements are thought provoking and open-ended—learners should need to respond with more than a simple yes or no.
   - Check to see if the statements are related to larger concepts or ideas rather than just isolated facts.
2. Write the statements, in order, down the centre of the page.
3. On the left side of each statement, leave a blank space for the student's response before reading; on the right side of the statement, leave a blank space for student's response after reading.
4. Before reading the passage, ask the student to place an *A* in the blank space on the left if he or she agrees with the statement or a *D* if he or she disagrees with the statement. Do this step orally to encourage the student to talk through ideas.
5. After the student has put an *A* or *D* beside each statement, ask the learner to explain the reasons for the choices. The discussion should give a good idea of the student's prior knowledge of the topic in the selection before reading begins.
6. Have the student read the passage independently, or read the passage with the student. Your degree of involvement will be determined by student fatigue, engagement, and passage difficulty.
7. Once the reading is finished, ask the student to complete the second column, with an *A* for agree and a *D* for disagree.
8. Together, compare the before-reading responses with the after-reading responses. Encourage the student to support responses with references to the text.

An example of an anticipation guide for an article on cloning might look something like this:

Anticipation Guide for "A Clone in Sheep's Clothing"

To the student: Before reading this article, take a few minutes to think about your reaction to each of the following statements. Indicate each of your responses in the space to the left of each statement. Write an *A* if you agree, a *D* if you disagree. After you have read the passage, repeat the process. Note your agreement or disagreement in the column on the right side of the page. Be prepared to discuss the reasons for your responses with your tutor.

Before Reading   After Reading

1. _____   Cloning holds enormous promise for the human race.   _____

2. _____   Cloning is cruel to animals.   _____

3. _____   Cells from adult animals can't be used to make a new animal.   _____

4. _____   Cloned animals are prone to disease.   _____

Probable Passage

Probable Passage is a reading strategy which encourages students to become involved in reading a text by making predictions, learning new vocabulary, and seeing relationships among key concepts (Beers 2003). The teacher chooses words that represent important ideas in a text. The tutor then presents them to the student, discusses what they mean, and helps the student arrange the words into categories. For fictional texts, the categories could include character, setting, problem, solution, and unknown words. For informational texts, categories could be what, where/location, process, results, and unknown words. The categories may need to shift for informational texts, depending on the subject area: the teacher can guide the tutor in choosing appropriate categories for a given reading.

By helping students think about main ideas and vocabulary, Probable Passage encourages dependent readers to take a more active role in the reading process (Wood 1984). It encourages learners to use what they know about the structure of stories and informational texts, develop their vocabulary, make predictions, and feel comfortable admitting that they don't know what some words mean. Also since it may involve using envelopes and placing words on slips of paper within them, Probable Passage appeals to kinesthetic learners.

Although originally developed as a whole-class activity, Probable Passage can be easily adapted to a tutoring situation. As tutors become more experienced, they will find that the structure of Probable Passage enables different conversation and connections to be made. As always, teachers play an important role in introducing tutors to the strategy and supplying them with examples and directions.

1. Before meeting the student and with teacher guidance, the tutor makes a list of 10 to 14 key words from the story about to be read. The words should cover characters, setting, problem, and outcome; there should also be a few difficult words that the student is likely to place in the Unknown Words box. Of course, if an informational text is about to be read, then the words should cover other appropriate categories, such as what, where/location, how, why, and unknown words. It always helps to choose some difficult words from the upcoming passage so that the student will feel comfortable admitting when a word is not understood.

Characters	*Setting*	*Problem*	*Solution*	*Unknown Words*

2. Before meeting the student, the tutor labels small boxes or envelopes—Characters, Setting, Problem, Solution, and Unknown Words—and writes key words on slips of paper.

3. The tutor asks the student to place the words in the appropriate boxes or envelopes. The tutor needs to know and to stress that there is no one right box or envelope for a word; rather, it is important to hear how the student makes sense of each word and its relationship to the category.

Students benefit when they and their tutors return to the prediction sentences after reading. They can discuss the accuracy of their predictions, answer earlier raised questions, and define or explain the unknown words from story context.

4. The tutor should model how to do this. For instance, the tutor could say, "I'd place this word, 'Carolina,' in Setting because I know there is a place called Carolina. Then again, it could also go into the Characters envelope because it could be the name of a girl in the story." It is important for the tutor to demonstrate that words can have more than one meaning, depending on context. This demonstration makes the student feel comfortable making guesses.

5. The tutor invites the student to say out loud the reasons behind placing each word in the selected boxes or envelopes.

6. The tutor then asks the student to use a few of the words to make a one-sentence prediction about the story. The tutor can help the student get started by providing a prompt, perhaps "I think I'm going to read about …" The tutor writes down the sentence generated by the student.

7. The tutor asks the student what he or she hopes to find out by reading the story or informational text. The tutor records the questions generated by the student.

8. Finally, the tutor asks the student to predict the title of the selection and records that prediction.

A Probable Passage can be created for reading a history text using the same box categories as listed above. If content-area texts are being used, it is prudent for teachers to play a role here, indicating the ideas and details on which they would like the tutor to focus.

In addition, Probable Passage can be used with science, geography, and mathematics readings, so long as the tutor can generate new categories. For example, a geography textbook discussing altitude and air masses could have envelopes labelled What, Where/Location, Process, Results, and Unknown Words. (See next page for a complete geography example.) For a science passage describing human digestion, box labels could be Body Part, Function, Action on Food/Nutrient, Location, Process, and Unknown Words. Category labels for a mathematics passage might be Formula, Symbols, Actions, and Unknown Words.

A non-fiction model for Probable Passage appears as an appendix. Here is an example of how a tutor and student might handle a content-area passage.

Probable Passage: Non-Fiction Model

Title of Selection: _____

Envelopes labelled with categories

| What | Where/ Location | Process | Results | Unknown Words |

Slips of paper with key words from the text

| atmosphere | | condenses | | orographic precipitation | | altitude | | moisture |

| windward side | | rain shadow | | rain | | snow | | air masses |

| mountain chains | | winds |

Slips of paper placed into appropriate envelopes

| What | Where/ Location | Process | Results | Unknown Words |

Pre-reading Strategies at Work

The strategies presented in this chapter may be used by a teacher or a tutor to prepare a student for reading. They include focus questions, K-W-L charts, content analysis, graphic organizers, anticipation guides, and Probable Passages. Although each strategy is unique, it has features in common with the other strategies. All of them encourage positive interaction between the tutor and the student. They help the student prepare to make meaning of the focus text for the session. Also most of them involve some visual component that helps the student conceptualize the key concepts, ideas, and terms dealt with in the text.

The recommended strategies are very flexible. Each can be used to accomplish a variety of pre-reading goals, such as activating prior knowledge, visualizing concepts, engaging the reader with the text, pre-teaching vocabulary, and making predictions.

Okay, Let's Start

In the sample dialogue, notice how the tutor engages the student in the text by helping her make personal connections to the topic. Notice, too, how the tutor explains the technique in the context of the text about to be read.

Tutor: For our session today, your science teacher has asked me to help you with this article on cloning. Do you know what that is?

Student: I saw something on television about cloning. Didn't somebody make a copy of a sheep?

Tutor: That's right. Her name was Dolly. Cloning is a process used to reproduce identical copies of a living organism. It could be a plant or an animal.

Student: Could they make a copy of my dog?

Tutor: It's possible.

Student: How do they that?

Tutor: Well, let's see if we can find the answer to your question in the article.

Student: Okay.

Tutor: Before we begin, I'd like to hear what you think about cloning. I have a little activity we can do together. (*Tutor takes out anticipation guide.*)

Student: What's that?

Tutor: The fancy name for it is an anticipation guide, but really it's just a way for you to say what you think about a subject before you read what the author says. I've written out some sentences that deal with the topic of cloning. On the right-hand side is a space. I'm going to ask you to write an *A* if you agree with the statement and a *D* if you disagree. There is no right or wrong answer so just write what you think and then we'll talk about it.

Student: Are you going to put down your opinion too?

Tutor: Sure, and then we'll compare answers.

Student: What are the blanks on the other side for?

Tutor: Well, when we're done reading the passage, we'll see if we've changed our minds and we can talk about whether we agree or disagree with what the author says.

Student: Okay, let's start.

Chapter 7 Helping Students While They Read

The challenge facing tutors is to find ways to teach the strategies that they use automatically while they read to students who do not use them, and the challenge for teachers is to help tutors make the automatic conscious. This chapter outlines many strategies tutors can teach students to use while they read and suggests ways for teachers to support tutors in these processes.

Tutoring as Thoughtful Talk

Tutoring is not a silent process. One of the most important things that tutors can do is to model, make visible, and reinforce the habits of mind used by successful readers. To this end, tutors should talk regularly during tutoring sessions to demonstrate their own thought processes as they read with and to their students. They will need to model and regularly explain what they do as effective readers. They externalize what for independent readers is an internal and automatic process. Through the communication bag and in face-to-face meetings, teachers are wise to remind tutors to do this and to model it themselves, particularly in the first month of tutoring.

During the act of reading, the brains of independent readers are engaged with text. Independent readers are constantly trying to make sense of what they are reading. If there are parts they don't understand, they reread the passages. They have silent conversations with the author to identify those things with which they agree or disagree. They turn the words on the page into images in their heads and visualize what is happening in a story or what the author is explaining to them in an article. As they use their own experiences to confirm or challenge what they are reading, they are constantly making personal connections with the text.

Dependent readers do not engage the text in the same way. They lack a repertoire of strategies to create meaning out of the symbols on the page. They may not even realize that such strategies are available to help them understand what they are reading. That is why tutor modelling during the time that tutors and students spend together is so important in helping the students acquire a range of effective reading strategies.

There are several important instructional goals for the during-reading part of the lesson. The strategies used during reading will help learners

During-reading strategies enable readers to

- check understanding
- make predictions
- monitor meaning
- clarify confusion
- make personal connections
- visualize what they read
- make inferences

Based on Beers (2003)

understand the text and deal effectively with those parts they do not understand. By making predictions and checking them against what the author says, they make reading an increasingly active process. By taking time to visualize what they read, students learn how to use their senses to enhance the meanings of the words, phrases, and sentences before them.

As with pre-reading, specific reading strategies can help learners achieve the goals of effective reading. In this chapter, several strategies that have proven to be particularly effective in helping students become independent during reading are explained. The strategies are flexible and can be adapted to achieve more than one reading objective. Each has been adapted to a tutoring situation. Sometimes in a single 45-minute session, there is time only for pre-reading and during-reading activities. If the text being read is longer, spanning several tutoring sessions, tutors will spend most time on activities associated with the stage of reading completion. For instance, if a tutor and student are just starting a text, the majority of time will be spent on pre-reading strategies. If a text is completed during a session, tutors will move the activities into after-reading strategies.

Of utmost importance is balancing tutoring time between readings needed for courses and readings that appeal to student interests. Overarching tutoring goals pertain to improving self-confidence and motivation as well as reading skills: research reminds us of the importance of choosing topics of interest to do this, particularly for males.

Focus Questions with During-Reading Goals

Posing questions during the reading phase helps tutors determine how well their students understand the text. By answering these questions, students determine what they do not understand and what they need to clarify. Questions can also be used to help students make personal connections with the text, to relate to what is happening in a story, and to respond to ideas proposed by an author.

In one-to-one situations, tutors can make effective use of questions to determine the decoding and comprehension strategies that students are able to use and those that are new to them. By modelling techniques that students are not yet able to use, tutors help expand the personal reading repertoires of their students. Dependent readers need to know that fluent readers ask questions while they read to create their own meaning—they are interacting with the text.

The chart on page 85 provides examples of questions that could be asked to support the goals of instruction during reading. Tutors would benefit from having a copy of it.

Although questions stimulate thinking and invite reflection, tutors need to know about the problem of overusing them. Interfering with the natural flow of a selection—the fluency—may interfere with the reader's ability to obtain meaning from the text. Asking a few well-placed questions, at natural pauses in the reading process, is far better than interrupting the reading with many questions. Tutors should also be aware that one goal of asking questions is to prompt students to learn to ask their own questions while reading.

Questions to Ask During Reading

Reading Goals	Narrative Texts	Informational Texts
Make predictions	What do you think is going to happen next? What clues does the author give you about what is going to happen next?	How could this information be used? What might be the next section or sub-heading in this article?
Check for understanding	What has happened so far in the story? What do you think this word means?	In your own words, explain the author's main idea. If you could ask the author a question about this topic, what would it be?
Monitor meaning	What do you think the character means when he/she says "_____"? What is another word the character might have used in this sentence?	Why did the author include _____ in the article? How do you know this is non-fiction?
Clarify confusion	What did you find confusing in the last paragraph? What words are new to you?	What words did you find confusing? What ideas do you wish the author had explained more clearly?
Make personal connections	What went through your mind when …? How did you feel when the character …?	What new thing have you learned so far in this selection? How does this information connect to your life or what you know already?
Visualize what is being read	What did you see in your imagination when you were reading this part of the story?	What are you seeing in your mind as you read this? How could the information in this article be used to make a picture or graphic?

Modelled Questioning

When independent readers read a text, they constantly ask their own questions, for their own reasons, based on their own interests. Strategic, independent readers ask questions to clarify confusion, to wonder (extend the information given), and to critically analyse.

Tutors can model how to ask questions while reading, sometimes to note a confusion, sometimes to wonder where to find out more information, and sometimes to debate an idea expressed by an author. Initially, teachers will need to model this for tutors. Once they see the kind of thinking aloud that is involved, tutors quickly pick up the concept. Sample questions that tutors might use follow.

To note confusion:
- What does this word mean?
- What is this sentence telling me?
- Why is that graphic on this page? How does it relate to the words and content?

To wonder or extend information:
- I'm interested in this fact on this sidebar. I wonder where I could find more information?
- I wonder if the suspect in this crime will be found?
- I wonder why families argue?

To debate an idea:
- Whose voice is missing in this text?
- Why did this news story interview only people who were in favor of the expansion of this highway?
- Where did the author get these facts?

Once tutors have modelled asking a question, then they can support students in learning to ask their own questions. Here is an example of teaching students how to ask questions to get meaning from a text.

Tutor: When you were reading that last sentence out loud, I noticed that you stumbled over the word "inconsolable."
Student: Yeah, it's got too many letters.
Tutor: Do you know what it means?
Student: Not really.
Tutor: You know what I do sometimes when I come across a word I don't know?
Student: What?
Tutor: I ask myself some questions.
Student: Out loud?
Tutor: No, not out loud, but inside my head.
Student: You mean you talk to yourself?
Tutor: In a way I do, especially when I'm answering my own questions.
Student: What do you mean?
Tutor: Well, let's take the word "inconsolable" as an example. First, I might ask myself, "What's the word about? Who is it describing?"
Student: The girl?

Tutor: Right. Then, I might ask myself, "What is the author telling me about the girl?"

Student: I don't have a clue.

Tutor: Well, let's look at the next sentence to see if we can find one. Read it out loud for me.

Student: "She moped around for days and nothing anyone could do would cheer her up."

Tutor: Try asking yourself a question that gets at the meaning of what you've just read.

Student: "What's that matter with her?"

Tutor: Good one. Now find an answer to your own question and before you know it, you'll be talking to yourself just like me.

Student: She's not very happy. She's just moping around.

Tutor: Good. Can you take a guess now at what *inconsolable* means?

Student: No one can cheer her up?

Tutor: Exactly.

Tutors can guide students as they ask questions while reading, and together, they can notice if the text offers answers to the questions. Of course, if students raise questions based on confusion, tutors need to support them in finding clues to answer the questions right away. The deeper questions that deal with extending information and critical thinking are often highly complex and sometimes unanswerable. As in other cases, questions may be oral or written by hand or, if possible, listed on a computer where they can easily be saved and used later.

Story and Sequence Maps, Fishbone Charts, and T-charts

Graphic organizers are effective tutoring tools not only before reading, but also during reading. Tutors may use organizers such as story maps to achieve a variety of during-reading instructional goals. These include

- checking for understanding
- making predictions
- clarifying confusion
- making personal connections
- visualizing what is being read

For purposes of illustration, each of the examples below focuses on a single during-reading instructional goal. Any one graphic organizer may, however, be used for a variety of purposes.

Our research shows that computer programs, including basic word-processing programs, can be helpful and engaging for creating graphic organizers, particularly for boys.

Story and Sequence Maps

A **story map** is a visual display of the elements of a narrative text. Typical elements of a story map include the main characters, setting (time and place), main events in the plot (or problems faced by the main characters), climax, resolution, theme, and author's purpose. Initially, the teacher may need to be involved in selecting these elements, but increasingly tutors will be able to do this on their own. The elements selected by the tutor should be appropriate to the student's needs, age, and level of understanding. In all cases, these elements are arranged in a series of boxes that are filled in by the learner, with the help of the tutor, as they are discovered during the reading of the text.

A simplified version of a story map might look much like that for "The Scream," shown on "Story Maps: What They Look Like" (see the Appendixes for blank versions). Story maps that incorporate more of the elements above would be used for texts at a more difficult reading level. The reproducible aid to tutors also shows the variations of plot map and news story map.

A **sequence map** is similar to a story map, but used with informational rather than narrative texts. It might include the elements of a process, the arguments used to support a thesis, or the components of an explanation. As with the story map, the sequence map is a visual depiction of the relationships among the structural elements of non-fiction. Typical elements include main topics and subtopics; thesis and supporting evidence; headings and subheadings; or introduction, main body, and conclusion.

A sequence map for a scientific or geographic process might look something like that on how the ear works. For an essay, it might look like the example on garbage.

Story or sequence maps can be used by following these steps:

1. Before the tutoring session, the tutor receives from the teacher or prepares a map which includes the generic components of the chosen story or article and shows how they are connected visually. These will be lines, cells, or boxes in which the learner will later write specifics of the story or article.

2. The tutor and the student discuss the purpose of a map: to give directions for reaching a specific destination. The tutor can then explain how this map applies to the reading.

3. The student and the tutor begin to read the selection.

4. As the student discovers the various components of the map, the tutor provides prompts for filling in the details in the appropriate sections.

5. During reading, the tutor and the student use the map to check for understanding and to clarify any confusion.

6. After reading, they use it to discuss the main ideas and the student's personal response to them.

Story Maps: What They Look Like

Example of a Story Map—Simplified Version

"The Scream" by Diana J. Wieler

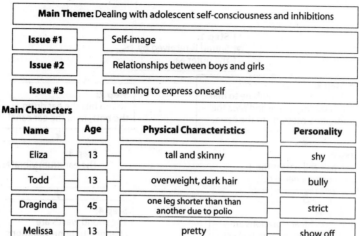

Main Theme: Dealing with adolescent self-consciousness and inhibitions

Issue #1	Self-image
Issue #2	Relationships between boys and girls
Issue #3	Learning to express oneself

Main Characters

Name	Age	Physical Characteristics	Personality
Eliza	13	tall and skinny	shy
Todd	13	overweight, dark hair	bully
Draginda	45	one leg shorter than than another due to polio	strict
Melissa	13	pretty	show off

Example of a Plot Map for "The Scream"

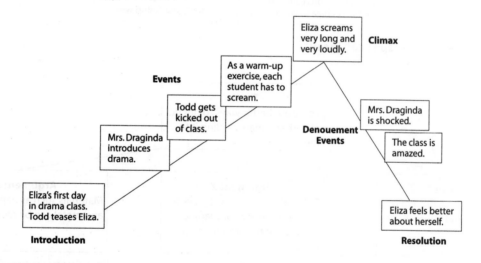

Eliza's first day in drama class. Todd teases Eliza. **Introduction**

Mrs. Draginda introduces drama.

Todd gets kicked out of class.

As a warm-up exercise, each student has to scream. **Events**

Eliza screams very long and very loudly. **Climax**

Denouement Events

Mrs. Draginda is shocked.

The class is amazed.

Eliza feels better about herself. **Resolution**

Example of a News Story Map

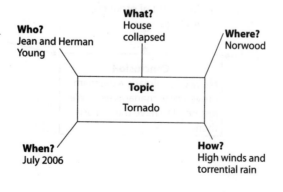

Who? Jean and Herman Young

What? House collapsed

Where? Norwood

Topic Tornado

When? July 2006

How? High winds and torrential rain

Sequence Maps: What They Look Like

Example of a Sequence Map Showing a Process

Topic: How the ear works

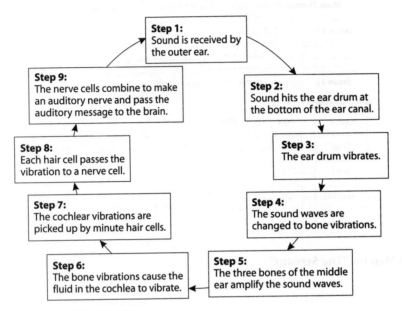

Example of a Sequence Map for an Essay

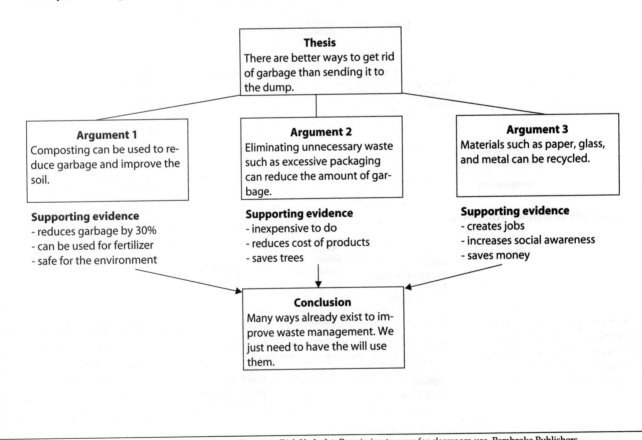

Fishbone or Herringbone Charts

This type of organizer works well with informational texts.

As the name suggests, a **fishbone** or **herringbone chart** is a graphic organizer that resembles the skeleton of a fish. Consider the head and the spine of the fish as the main idea, while the fins and bones represent the subsidiary ideas. This kind of organizer is often used to help learners solve problems or to identify and organize ideas (Bennett and Rolheiser 2001).

In a tutoring situation, a herringbone chart can be used in all stages of the reading process, but is particularly useful in the during-reading stage as a tool to help dependent readers understand the key concepts and ideas presented in an informational text. In an explanatory piece of prose, for example, the concept explained by the author becomes the head and spine, the key aspects of the main idea are the fins, while the explanatory details and examples are the bones. Herringbone charts become ineffective if too many ideas are included. The components are arranged in a visual such as this:

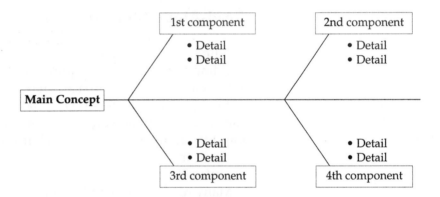

The tutor and the learner complete such a chart as follows:

1. They fill in the main concept on the fish's spine.

2. They fill in the major components on the fins.

3. They then fill in the details.

4. The tutor begins by doing the first component as an example.

5. The tutor and the student complete the rest together. During the process, the tutor checks for understanding, clarifies any confusion, and discusses with the student how the components relate to the main concept and to one another.

T-charts

T-charts work well with any text, fiction or informational, where comparisons are being made or where different sides of an issue are being debated.

As the name suggests this graphic organizer is in the shape of a large "**t**." It is used to visualize responses to a story or to informational text. The vertical line of the **t** divides the page into two columns. The spaces at the top, one to the right and another to left of the place where the two lines intersect, are used for the topics being compared. The spaces below the horizontal line are used for details. Kinds of comparisons might include the following:

91

- What I know/What I need to know
- What I like/What I don't like
- Questions I have/Possible answers
- What I understand/What I don't understand
- Problems/Solutions
- Benefits/Drawbacks
- Pros/Cons

Benefits	Drawbacks

Before beginning to read the passage with the learner, the tutor explains or determines, with the help of the learner, the purpose of the activity: for example, to understand the main ideas of the selection, to clarify what the author is saying, or to respond to the author's ideas. As the tutor and learner read the passage, they complete the two sides of the t-chart together. When they have finished reading the passage, they use the information on the chart to discuss the objective identified at the beginning.

Read-Aloud Strategies

Reading aloud has been called the single most important activity for building the knowledge required for success in reading (Anderson et al. 1985). Oral reading approaches have proven to be particularly successful with dependent readers (Beers 2003). The approaches described below can be used to build confidence, increase fluency, achieve accuracy, and improve **automaticity**, or the ability to see a word and automatically know its meaning. They can also make reading fun for both the tutor and the tutored.

Many read-aloud activities involve pairs sharing the work of reading and, therefore, readily lend themselves to tutoring situations. Some of the more commonly used approaches are echo reading, repeated reading, partner reading, reading in unison, and reading to each other.

Echo Reading

Learners will benefit most when they hear tutors use their voices in a dramatic manner, focusing on effective phrasing and clear enunciation. When tutors do this, it creates interest, motivates dependent readers, and promotes understanding.

In **echo reading**, the tutor reads aloud one or two sentences and the learner repeats what the tutor has read, mimicking the tutor's speech patterns. Imitating intonation and pacing helps the learner acquire the skills used by fluent readers.

Repeated Reading

It is important that texts for repeated reading be ones that the student enjoys, which reinforces the pleasure of reading.

In **repeated reading**, the learner reads and rereads familiar passages or parts of favorite books. By returning to the same material over time, the learner begins to recognize textual features, such as headings and subheadings, which guide the reader. This approach also helps the reader become increasingly aware of the relationship between symbols and sounds, thus increasing fluency. This tutoring strategy encourages confidence and fluency.

Partner Reading

In **partner reading**, the tutor and the student take turns reading so that the student can hear parts of the text read fluently and have a short break from reading. Listening to an effective oral reading also improves the student's ability to gain meaning from what is read. Taking turns reading out loud helps students anticipate the words and ideas they will encounter when it becomes their turn to read.

Partner reading helps ensure that dependent readers will complete the reading of a given text. Often, they do not complete long or difficult texts, something that compounds problems with comprehension as well as with their self-confidence and self-esteem.

Reading in Unison

The tutor and the student sit side by side and read the selection aloud in unison. **Reading in unison** allows the student to read chunks of text at one sitting and to readily get meaning from what is read. It also helps the student build fluency and share in the pleasure and satisfaction of reading. When reading together, the tutor models the correct pronunciation of words, clarifies the meaning of unfamiliar words, and maintains a reading pace conducive to making meaning of the text.

Reading to Each Other

Either the student or the tutor reads part of the text first. The listener then retells the selection that has just been read or the reader asks questions about the selection. The kinds of questions that are asked will depend on the goal of the tutoring session, perhaps making personal connections or identifying important detail. The reader and the student then reverse roles. Dependent readers often enjoy finding questions that will stump their tutors.

Think Alouds

Dependent readers will need regular opportunities to think aloud to help internalize the thinking process and have it become automatic. From time to time, tutors could ask their students how thinking out loud changes their reading habits.

Think aloud is a key strategy for helping students who struggle with comprehension to make inferences and draw personal connections (Tovani 2000). **Think alouds** make explicit what independent readers do subconsciously to obtain meaning from what they read. Independent readers think about what they are reading; in fact, they realize that reading *is* thinking. Dependent readers, however, do not do so. They do not note what they fail to understand, and therefore, they do not think about strategies to make sense out of a text. Think alouds help dependent readers learn to think about what they are reading. The technique lends itself well to a tutoring situation.

The following sequence map shows how the think aloud process can be used by tutors to help the learners with whom they are working.

Modelling the Think Aloud Process

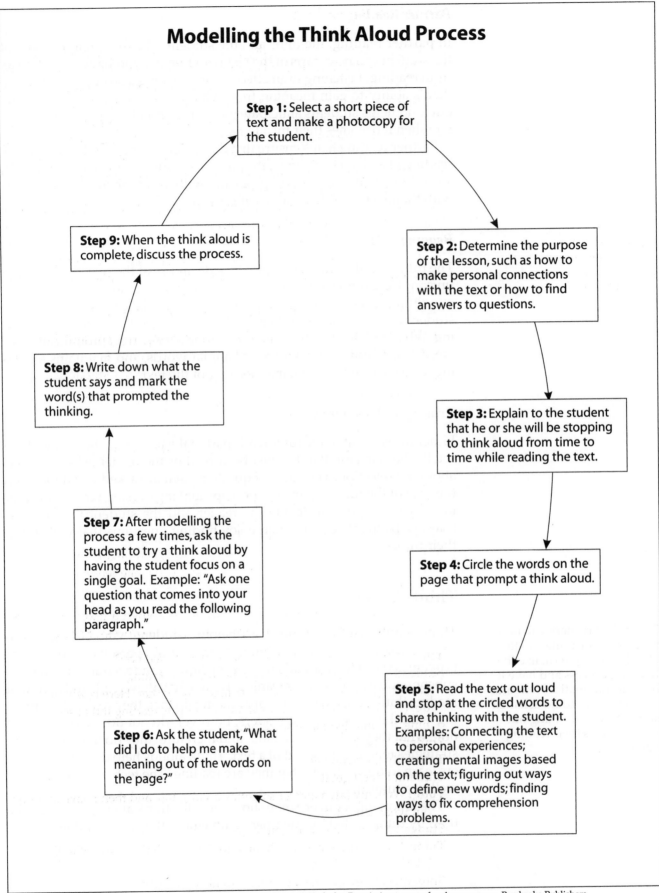

Step 1: Select a short piece of text and make a photocopy for the student.

Step 2: Determine the purpose of the lesson, such as how to make personal connections with the text or how to find answers to questions.

Step 3: Explain to the student that he or she will be stopping to think aloud from time to time while reading the text.

Step 4: Circle the words on the page that prompt a think aloud.

Step 5: Read the text out loud and stop at the circled words to share thinking with the student. Examples: Connecting the text to personal experiences; creating mental images based on the text; figuring out ways to define new words; finding ways to fix comprehension problems.

Step 6: Ask the student, "What did I do to help me make meaning out of the words on the page?"

Step 7: After modelling the process a few times, ask the student to try a think aloud by having the student focus on a single goal. Example: "Ask one question that comes into your head as you read the following paragraph."

Step 8: Write down what the student says and mark the word(s) that prompted the thinking.

Step 9: When the think aloud is complete, discuss the process.

Modelled Rereading

Rereading is probably the strategy most used by skilled readers and *least* used by dependent readers (Tovani 2000). Independent readers assume that it is their job to construct meaning from a text; dependent readers often do not try to figure out what a text means. Dependent readers do not believe that rereading does them any good. They assume that skilled readers read something once and "get it" the first time. That is not the case. Skilled readers pause, loop back up a few sentences, reread to a point, reflect, start over completely, or proceed more slowly. Dependent readers cannot see this happening.

The task of tutors is to model rereading for students and demonstrate clearly and convincingly that this strategy not only works for them, but will also work for the students. Tutors need to talk with their students about how often they reread, why they reread, how rereading differs from reading something for the first time, and how to choose which sections need rereading.

Tutors may take the following steps to achieve this goal:

> The task of tutors is to show students clearly and convincingly that rereading is a strategy that works for them and will work for the students.

1. The tutor introduces rereading by showing the student how this strategy allows skilled readers to discover things in a text they did not see on a first reading or how to clarify confusion. For example:

Tutor: You seemed to stumble a bit on that last sentence. What do you think the author was trying to tell you?
Student: I have no idea.
Tutor: What do you usually do when you come to a part you don't understand?
Student: I skip it.
Tutor: (*laughs*) Actually, sometimes that's not a bad idea, as long as it still makes sense. Have you tried rereading it?
Student: You mean read it again? What for?
Tutor: Well, by reading something a second time, you can discover things you didn't see the first time or it might help you make sense of something that was confusing.

2. The tutor models the thinking that occurs when a text is reread by explaining out loud what happens during the process. For example:

Tutor: What was it in the last sentence that confused you?
Student: I didn't get the part about the dirt bike stalling.
Tutor: Well, you know, I wasn't sure about that either. Here is what I would do. (*Tutor rereads the sentence out loud*). As I was reading it that second time, it reminded me of something.
Student: What?
Tutor: My lawn mower.
Student: I don't get it.
Tutor: Well, my lawn mower sometimes stalls, too, and then I have to figure out what caused it.
Student: You mean like it's out of gas?
Tutor: That would make it stall for sure! But was that the case with the dirt bike?
Student: No, because he didn't have to fill it with gas.

Tutor: Right! So then I would ask myself, "What else could cause the stalling?" Is there anything that would give us a hint in that last sentence?

Student: He went through water. Maybe, the starter got wet or some water got into the gas line.

Tutor: Brilliant! You know more about dirt bikes than I do! You see how you can use what you already know to figure out something that you don't?

Student: I get it.

3. The tutor then asks the student to read and then reread, once or twice, a short text. The text could be as short as a sentence or part of a sentence. Usually, it will take at least a paragraph so that the student can determine meaning from the context of the other sentences.

4. For each rereading, the tutor gives the student a specific task or purpose. For example, if looking at a geography text, the tutor might say, "Notice any visual clues that help you understand how to see a cold front.… Notice any clues that suggest what words are most important when reading about a cold front."

5. After each rereading, the tutor asks the student to rate how well he or she understood the text on a scale of 1 to 10 and discusses reasons for changes in the rating.

6. The tutor and the student brainstorm how rereading is helpful and discuss the circumstances under which it can be used.

As with think alouds, the key to internalizing the rereading strategy is regular practice. The tutor needs to model the strategy at each tutoring session, especially once the idea of rereading has been introduced. Similarly, whenever the student has a problem with making meaning from a text, rereading should be one of the first strategies used.

Be Aware of Instructional Goals

The strategies in this chapter can be used by a teacher or a tutor to help a student obtain meaning from a text during the reading process. They include using questions, either those posed by the tutor or by the student, to check for understanding; using graphic organizers to visualize the content of the text; using read-aloud strategies to develop comprehension and fluency; doing think alouds to make the reader consciously aware of reading strategies; and rereading to clarify confusion and construct meaning.

For purposes of illustration, each of the strategies outlined in this chapter has been linked to a goal appropriate to the during-reading part of the reading process: these include making predictions, checking for understanding, monitoring meaning, clarifying confusion, making personal connections, making inferences, and visualizing what has been read. It is important to remember, however, that all of these strategies can be used to achieve any of the other goals. When selecting strategies, tutors need to be aware of instructional goals. The classroom teacher will need to clarify the reading goals that are important for each of the students being tutored and to help tutors select strategies that best meet those goals.

Chapter 8 Helping Students After They Read

After-reading strategies enable the reader to

- clarify meaning
- demonstrate understanding
- make personal connections
- summarize information
- identify main ideas and issues
- see causal connections
- draw conclusions

Based on Beers (2003)

Tutor responsibilities do not end when a book is closed. Tutors can help dependent readers derive further meaning from a text through the activities that follow the reading itself. They can show students how to gain further meaning from the text, as well as to find ways to respond personally to it. This part of the tutoring lesson also provides tutors with an excellent opportunity to use their own enthusiasm to motivate students to keep on reading.

The amount of time spent on this phase will depend on how much time has already been spent on other activities. In a 45-minute session, if the student completes the reading within the first 10 to 15 minutes, the tutor might spend 20 minutes more on this phase, reserving the last 10 minutes for focus on reading in the student's area of interest. The tutor might well return to the after-reading activities in the following session. The decision will depend on the importance of the text—it might be a text that is important in the content area—or on the engagement of the student being tutored. If students feel that they have done all they wish to do on a particular text, it is time to move on.

Our research shows that dependent readers rate talking about what they have read as their least favorite reading activity. Yet, fluent readers stay engaged with text after reading it through thinking or talking about what they have read. They continue to think about what's been read, make judgments about what the author told them, reflect upon what the text means for them, and simply enjoy the pleasure and sense of satisfaction that come from having read an interesting text. When they finish reading, skilled readers tend to talk about what they have read and begin reading another text that interests them. There are two options for post-reading engagement. Tutors may choose aspects of the text that students find interesting or surprising, being sure to work from students' interests; or, they may vary the post-reading activities, to include kinesthetic responses, mapping exercises, and use of the computer.

As with the first two stages of the reading process, the post-reading phase focuses on a number of instructional goals. Although the tutor has been helping the student make sense of the text throughout the reading process, the student may still have questions about some parts of the text. Now is a good time for the tutor to clarify any confusion that remains in the student's mind. The tutor may also bring the tutoring session to a close with a review of key information, the story's main events, or the article's central ideas. Additional practice in essential reading skills, such as summarizing and drawing conclusions, may be provided, as well. Finally, by helping the student make causal connections within the text and personal connections with the text, the tutor can help the reader both to respond to the current text and to prepare for the next reading experience.

Activities that follow the reading of a text help the student consolidate what has been learned. The post-reading phase is also the time to check the accuracy of predictions made by the student in the before-reading part of the lesson. Discrepancies can now be corrected by rereading pertinent portions of a text.

Tutors may wish to discuss the text in a way that supports vocabulary building, use of decoding skills, and additional practice in comprehension. For instance, tutors might reinforce new vocabulary by going back to the new words identified in the before-reading activities and, through brief quizzing, demonstrate to students what they have learned. Or, tutors might have students identify root words and prefixes and suffixes found in the passage. (See Chapter 10 for more ideas.) To build motivation, it is recommended that tutors focus on those aspects of the text that students found interesting and compelling. If a student is intrigued by the fact that the image projected on the retina of the human eye is initially upside down before the brain turns the image right side up, for example, the tutor might return to that fact and do a wondering or extension activity with the concept, even working with the student to look up more information on the Internet. During the post-reading activities, it is important to maintain and build upon the enthusiasm and energy that will have resulted from a positive, shared reading experience.

Focus Questions with After-Reading Goals

A few carefully placed probing questions after reading allow the tutor to determine whether or not any further clarification is needed. (See the chart on page 99.) The tutor can ask the learner to briefly summarize—orally, by drawing, or by using the computer—what has been read or to identify the main ideas, events, and characters. The tutor can also use questions to engage the learner in a discussion or in a role-play about the reading experience shared together.

Examples of questions that can be used at this point in the tutoring session and the goals that they address appear on the next page. These focus questions are merely a starting point: a natural conversation about ideas and reactions to a text is a powerful way to close a reading session. It is a wonderful opportunity for reflection and reaction.

Focus Questions to Ask After Reading

Reading Goals	Narrative Texts	Informational Texts
Clarify meaning and check for understanding	What are three important characteristics of … [one of the characters]? What part of the story do you still find a little confusing?	What did you think was the most difficult part of this selection? What could the author have done to make it easier to understand?
Summarize	In one sentence, summarize the story. In your own words, retell the main events in this story.	In one sentence, state the author's main idea. Retell some of the information the author gave to support his/her point of view.
Draw causal connections	What makes this selection a story? Why did … do …? Why did … say …? What could … have done differently? How would that have changed the ending of the story?	What makes this selection non-fiction? What does the author want the reader to do as a result of reading this? Would you do it? How?
Make personal connections	What was your favorite part of the story? Why? What did this story remind you of?	What is one idea with which you agree? Why? What is the most surprising piece of information you learned from this text? Why?
Draw conclusions and think critically	From whose perspective have we heard the story? How would the story change if a different character were telling the story?	What perspective or information has been left out of this article? Why do you think it was excluded? Why did the author end the selection this way?

Mind Maps and Venn Diagrams

Chapters 6 and 7 presented several graphic organizers and focused on their purpose in the first two phases of the reading process. Any of these organizers may also be used in the final phase to achieve post-reading objectives. For example, a story map could be used to summarize a story; a pyramid outline or a fishbone chart could be used to look at the structure of an essay; and a thought web could be used to stimulate personal responses to a story or textbook selection.

In this chapter, the ways that tutors might use mind maps and Venn diagrams to achieve goals appropriate to the after-reading part of a session are outlined. Teachers might communicate this to tutors by leaving samples in the canvas communication bag and asking them to try something similar with students. Or they might walk tutors through the creation of a mind map or Venn diagram in a face-to-face meeting.

Mind Maps

Excellent computer programs designed especially for this are *Kidspiration*, *Inspiration* and *Smart Ideas*. If available, their use would benefit students.

A **mind map** consists of a circle or bubble drawn in the centre of a page from which lines connect to other circles. Each circle contains a piece of the information contained in a text. The lines trace the connections among the various pieces. When considered as a whole, the circles and lines and the connections among them should help learners determine how the author has organized the selection. Different colors can be used to identify the parts that have something in common.

In after-reading activities, students and tutors may create two mind maps. If the student is unfamiliar with mind maps, the tutor should draw the initial map, talking aloud as items are identified and placed into circles. If the tutor has already modelled this process, the onus is on the student to suggest ideas. In a second mind map, the focus is on clumping like items into categories. Some categories may already exist as one of the ideas generated; other categories will need to be created to serve as an organizer for ideas. The best idea is for the student to do as much of the clumping as possible, while the tutor talks out loud to model the thinking processes involved and ensure completion before the student gets fatigued. The two samples that appear on "Mind Maps and Venn Diagrams: What They Look Like" are based on the use of *Inspiration* software.

Mind Maps and Venn Diagrams: What They Look Like

Examples of Initial and Second Mind Maps

In the first mind map, tutor and student note ideas on a central theme; in the second, the student clumps together as many related ideas as possible and the tutor models the thinking out loud.

Example of a Venn Diagram

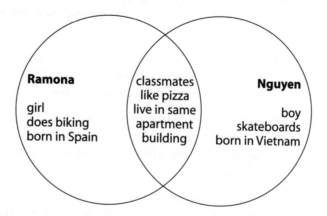

As students put similar items in the overlapping area and different items in the areas that do not overlap, they need to explain all their choices.

1. After the student reads an informational text, say, on life in pioneer times, the tutor prompts the student to look back at the text and, in a mind map format, write down all of the different aspects of life referred to by the author.

2. The tutor tells the student to circle all related items in colored pencil and to justify all decisions.

3. Next, the tutor asks the student to identify what the items have in common and to create a category heading for each circle of items. The student continues, with differently colored pencils, until all of the items have been placed into categories.

4. The student then creates a second mind map in which the categories become larger bubbles. The student writes the items that belong in each bubble. Doing this helps differentiate the categories, or types of things, that support the main idea from the specific examples.

5. Finally, the tutor asks the student to use the graphic to summarize the main points of the text and explain how they are connected.

Venn Diagrams

A **Venn diagram** consists of overlapping circles. It is used to show the similarities and differences between topics. The separate portions of the circles are filled with the distinct features or characteristics of each of the topics; the overlapping portion, with those they have in common.

After reading a selection that includes contrasting ideas, characters, events, places, theories, topics, and so on, the tutor may use a Venn diagram to encourage the reader to go back to the text and determine common features and differences between them.

This kind of activity not only directs the learner back to the text to confirm hypotheses about what has been read, but also encourages interaction with the information provided. It can be used to provide practice in drawing inferences, making comparisons, and reaching conclusions about the items being compared.

Tutors may create and use Venn diagrams as an after-reading activity in the following way.

1. Based on the student's interest and need, the tutor picks two characters from a story or two main ideas from an article and places them at the top of two overlapping circles.

2. The tutor explains that the student is going to place the characteristics or features that are in common in the area where the circles overlap and the ones that are unique to each of them in the areas that are distinct.

3. Together, tutor and student go back to the story or article and write the characteristics or features in the appropriate part of the diagram. Alternatively, the tutor could write the key items on cards or slips of paper ahead of time and have the student place them in the correct section of the diagram. The student is expected to justify all decisions.

Venn Diagram

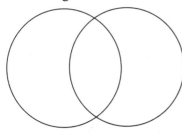

The student is expected to justify all decisions about where characteristics or features are placed in the Venn diagram.

Personal Response Activities

By encouraging the learner to make personal connections with the ideas, feelings, and experiences in a text, the tutor is able to help the reader gain further meaning from what has been read. The tutor can engage the learner emotionally and intellectually in a text through a variety of response activities. Only one activity is done per reading. Different activities take different amounts of time, and tutors need to judge how important a content text is or how strongly a student has engaged with texts in order to determine which activity to use. To ensure that they do not take an inordinate amount of time, these activities are often completed collaboratively.

Oral Response Activities

- Discuss personal responses to key moments, ideas, surprises, wonderings, and concerns.
- Role-play a section of dialogue.
- Debate an issue from the text.
- Improvise a scene from the story.

Visual Response Activities

- Draw a picture or create a comic of what has been read.
- Present the main ideas or events in a graphic.
- Find clip art from the Internet to create a poster of the main ideas.

Kinesthetic Response Activities

- Make something used by one of the characters in the story.
- Create a character box or an artifact box that contains items relevant to the character in a story or the topic/issue in an informational text.
- Draw or make a Plasticine model of an event, setting, or idea in a text.

If students are keeping response journals, tutors need to ensure that each time a new text is finished, students make brief entries about the text. Usually, tutors provide prompts, for example, "Would you recommend this text to a friend? Why or why not?"

Written Response Activities

- Keep a response journal.
- Turn a favorite part into a poem, song, or bumper sticker.
- Rewrite part of the text from a different point of view.

Frameworks to Summarize Text

After reading a text, skilled readers often summarize what they have read through discussion or retelling of text to friends or family. Summarizing helps them remember what they have read. Less skilled readers usually do not think about text after they have finished reading it. Yet, internalization of knowledge depends on remembering what has just been read.

The following frameworks help students learn how to summarize text so that they can better remember the main ideas of what they have read.

SWBS, or "Somebody Wanted But So," is a simple, four-column framework that demonstrates how to summarize a text (Beers 2003). The Somebody column encourages the learner to figure out the main character or group of people featured in the story or text. The Wanted column deals with motivations: what the "somebody" wanted. The But column focuses on the main conflicts. The So column examines resolutions and results.

Tutors may want to encourage their learners to come up with SWBS statements. In creating such statements, learners are able to use such skills as generalizing, seeing cause and effect, and identifying main ideas.

Using Frameworks for a Variety of Texts

Tutors can use the framework in a variety of ways for a variety of texts, including fiction and non-fiction.

For example, tutors could help learners to construct one sentence that covers the entire text or a series of sentences that cover various parts of the text. An SWBS for one scene of *Romeo and Juliet* would be: "The **Capulets and the Montagues** [somebody] **wanted** to kill each other, **but** Prince Escalus stepped in, and **so** peace was temporarily restored." A general version of an SWBS that covers the entire play might be, "**Romeo and Juliet wanted** to be together, **but** their parents and fate wouldn't allow it, **so** they both died tragically." SWBS can take what some people see as hard or challenging and boil it down to an understandable essence that they can easily remember.

The strategy can also be used to summarize an informational text. For example, an SWBS statement on the Winnipeg General Strike might read: "The **metal trade workers wanted** better working conditions, **but** the government and businesses wouldn't listen, **so** they went on strike, causing the Winnipeg General Strike."

Beyond helping learners summarize, this strategy can be used to help them understand point of view. By changing the character(s) in the Somebody column, the rest of the sentence changes. For example, if the term *government* were substituted into the Somebody column, the rest of the SWBS statement would change to reflect what the government wanted and what happened as a result.

Below are examples of SWBS-type charts that can be used for different kinds of texts.

Narrative or issue-based text			
Somebody	Wanted	But	So

Non-fiction text (Scientific or geographic)		
Something happens	Then this occurs	Which results in ...

Mathematical (and some scientific) texts			
Problem (State the problem and details given.)	**Concept** (What formula would apply?)	**Variables** (What do you know? What don't you know?)	**Result/Calculation** (Make all calculations and state results.)

Semantic Feature Analysis (SFA)

SFA is a powerful visual organizer that arranges new ideas and words in a logical, clear way for the learner (Fisher and Frey 2004). SFA is based on using a grid pattern to decide which features make up an idea. In the grid, terms or vocabulary comprise the rows while key features or characteristics make up the columns. In an informational text, the strategy helps learners understand content-area vocabulary used in a selection, assign features to ideas, organize, classify, and make comparisons between ideas.

The grid looks like this:

	Feature/Characteristic	Feature/Characteristic	Feature/Characteristic
Term			
Term			
Term			

A completed SFA chart for examining formation of rock in geography might look like this:

Rock Formation	Involves melting	Involves deposit from erosion	Involves change through pressure	Forms through a slow process	Results in very hard rock	Contains fossils
Sedimentary	–	+	–	+	–	+
Metamorphic	–	–	+	+	–	–
Igneous	+	–	–	–	+	–

Usually, the student completes the grid with the help of the tutor after reading the selection. The student places a plus sign in each cell to indicate that a relationship exists between the term and the feature or a minus sign when it is not a characteristic.

Personal Dictionaries or Word Boxes

It is helpful to students if tutors keep consistent track of any words that cause them difficulty while reading.

Many students who have problems with vocabulary and related fluency benefit from keeping personal dictionaries. To create personal dictionaries, students will need small notebooks. They enter one letter of the alphabet at the top of each page and add new vocabulary words onto the appropriate page. Teachers may ask tutors to initiate this process, or students may have already developed personal dictionaries, in which case, they would be expected to bring them to their tutoring sessions.

The tutor keeps track of words that caused difficulty for the student during the reading of a text. When the reading is finished, the tutor has the student write the words and their definitions in a book kept for the sole purpose of compiling a personal dictionary. Words must be arranged alphabetically by first letter so that the student can easily locate words and definitions.

An alternative is for the tutor to use cards that are kept on a key ring or in a box. The word is then written on the front of the card and the definition is written on the back. If cards are used, the tutor can create kinesthetic activities, such as asking the student to group the cards according to a specific characteristic (e.g., all nouns) or idea (e.g., all words with positive connotations). In addition, the tutor can encourage the student to create a classification system or show the interrelationship between the words in a visual manner. At the end of activities, the cards should be returned to alphabetic order for ease of later use.

From time to time during the tutoring sessions, tutors are wise to use the dictionary or box of words to review and practise students' new words. Consistent practice will allow students to increase their vocabularies dramatically. The more words students quickly recognize, the more their reading fluency improves.

Promote Enthusiasm

Engagement in after-reading activities helps students organize the texts they have read for deeper understanding. Using focus questions, graphic organizers, personal response, summarizing frameworks, and vocabulary building strategies will help students see relationships and connections more easily. These strategies will also take them back to the text for rereading, a habit of mind frequently used by skilled readers.

As always, tutor discretion and enthusiasm are critical in determining student energy levels and engagement. If a student becomes fatigued, it is better to finish the tutoring session with shared reading of an interesting text. Doing this reinforces the pleasure of reading and will help maintain student enthusiasm for tutoring. After-reading activities may be postponed to the next tutoring session.

Chapter 9 Resources That Support Tutoring

Matching the learner to appropriate texts is essential to successful tutoring. Many factors affect the choice of texts in a tutoring situation: interest, level of difficulty, personal experience, gender, family attitudes to reading, cultural background, and school context are among them.

Initially, classroom teachers will need to help with text selection; however, as tutors become more aware of the reading abilities and interests of their students, they will become better able to find engaging texts on their own. When tutors are using content-area texts, teacher involvement in text selection remains important: teacher priorities need to be addressed in the limited time available for tutoring. That said, for the part of the tutoring session that focuses on reading in areas of student interest, tutors often find texts of which teachers are unaware and many of these are superb. Tutors and teachers should expect there to be ongoing communication about text selection.

Some texts used will be at the student's *independent* reading level and some at the student's *instructional* reading level. The student should be asked to read texts at both levels in a tutoring session. Typically, a tutoring session begins with the student rereading familiar text or reading text at the student's independent reading level—the session starts on a positive note by enabling students to feel their own growth and capability as readers. Tutors should always have several different texts available, for students differ in energy and concentration ability on different days. Although ensuring that students tackle aspects of reading that they find difficult is important, tutors should choose which texts to use and which activities to do and for what duration of time guided by student energy.

Texts at Instructional and Independent Reading Levels: A Comparison

Instructional Level Text	Independent Level Text
• require tutor assistance • need help with word recognition • need help with comprehension	• require no tutor assistance • require almost complete word recognition • require high level of content comprehension

It is possible to quickly determine the readability of a text for a particular student. If the student can read 95–100 percent of the words accurately and comprehend without assistance at a level of 90 percent or more, then the text is at the student's independent (easy) reading level. Determining the reading level of a text begins with counting the number of words on the first page and determining what number would constitute 10 percent—the maximum number of errors allowed for a text that can be read independently. Then, as a student reads, the tutor simply counts the reading errors to determine whether the text is at an independent reading level or an instructional level, where tutor assistance is needed. Texts at an instructional level are used to teach and reinforce habits of mind that students are learning. Tutors will assist in the reading of these texts through before and during reading activities and by sharing the reading with students.

Some texts are even too difficult for use as instructional texts. Texts at the student's *frustrational* level—that is, texts where the student does not recognize 10 percent or more of the words and comprehends less than half of the ideas—should be avoided.

During the early tutoring sessions, it is advantageous for students to bring texts that they like and can read well. Students will gain in confidence and trust. For a variety of reasons, though, students may not bring in personal selections. Teachers need to alert tutors to be prepared for this and to bring in texts at different reading levels that might appeal to their students—tutors can select texts based on information in the "All About Me" inventory or the "Reading Interest and Attitude Survey."

As the tutoring progresses, students will reveal preferences, as well as strengths and needs. Once tutors become aware of student interests, needs, and reading level, decisions about which texts to use become easier. Ongoing communication between tutor and teacher will ensure that specific information about the student is exchanged regularly—to the benefit of teacher, tutor, and student alike.

Sources of Texts for Tutoring

Teachers are the logical first source of texts for tutoring. Until they learn about their students' reading abilities and areas of interest, tutors will benefit from teacher selection of text. As well, teachers must play a key role in choosing texts for content-area reading—and for clearly communicating expectations of focus areas and learning activities that the rest of the class may be doing. The teacher is not the only good source of texts, though: the students themselves, librarians, and tutors are also good sources for finding texts that will engage students.

Although some risks are involved in asking students to select texts—they may be too easy, too difficult, or inappropriate for the school context—significant insights into student strengths, needs, and interests can be gained by doing so. If tutors report that the text is difficult, teachers may gain insights into student needs. If the text a student brings is easy for the reader, it can be used to build confidence and improve fluency. If the text is inappropriate, it will provide an occasion to discuss the basis for text selection in future tutoring sessions.

Students learn best when they have texts that they *can* and *want* to read.

Be sure to remind tutors that sexually explicit, violent, or racist material is inappropriate for school reading. Advise them to notify you if a student brings in such material.

Text Sources from Home

Although some of the students being tutored may come from environments with few reading resources, the home is a potentially useful source of material. Parents and grandparents may give books as gifts to their children. Or students themselves might purchase favorite magazines, such as *Popular Mechanics* or *Seventeen.* Use of a favorite text is an excellent way to reinforce good reading strategies, provide motivation, and build confidence.

When a student brings texts from home, the tutor will gain important insights into the family culture. These insights, which should be passed on to the teacher, may point to the student's knowledge base and topics of interest. Success in reading is to a great extent based on what the student already knows. When students are prompted to talk about the topics and kinds of texts they read or would like to read, they draw upon the prior knowledge that is so critical to success in reading. A model tutor–student interaction follows.

Tutor: At our last session, you were telling me that you've started training your new puppy. How's it going?

Student: Molly's chewing everything! My baseball's a mess. I can't even find my socks.

Tutor: Sounds like she's teething. Might be a good time to read this article I brought with me.

Student: What's it about?

Tutor: It's about training your dog.

Student: Great!

Tutor: I bet you know quite a bit about training a dog already. One of the things they mention in the article is the importance of using rewards. Have you tried anything yet?

Student: Cheese.

Tutor: The author of the article says that food is one of the best motivators for training. What about time of day? When do you train Molly?

Student: After school.

Tutor: That fits well with another suggestion in the article. They suggest you train your dog before feeding her. I wonder why they suggest that?

Student: Then the food can be a reward?

Tutor: That's right.

Student: What else do they say?

Tutor: Let's find out!

Text Sources from Libraries

Classroom, school, and municipal libraries are usually the main sources of reading materials for tutoring sessions. Libraries are filled with texts that are age appropriate. Their shelves are stacked with books written about every subject imaginable and at levels of difficulty that are accessible to a wide range of learners. Once the student's independent and instructional reading levels are determined, the librarian becomes an excellent source of information about texts at appropriate levels of difficulty and interest. Librarians are also able to advise tutors about magazines and books that are popular with many students. This information will be invaluable, particularly for first-time tutors.

Especially as tutors get to know students' strengths, needs, and interests, they may become the most important sources of texts. Texts from popular culture, such as magazines, provide reading over multiple sessions and have high interest appeal. Tutors are best able to negotiate the gap between what students would like to read and what is available to them to read. When they remain alert to signals from students, tutors can play a key role in finding resources that students will find motivating and conducive to improvement in reading.

Benefits of Using Various Genres

Although research suggests that boys show preference for non-fiction over fiction, while with girls the reverse is true, it is wise to use a balance of genres in tutoring sessions.

Different genres offer different benefits to tutoring.

- For some learners, poetry is an excellent entry into reading. Poems are short, fun, and often deal with issues that engage adolescents. Poems, both narrative and lyrical, work well for activities in repeated reading and in expressive oral reading.
- Lyrics from popular songs are an excellent way to activate the prior knowledge that is so important for developing and reinforcing decoding and word recognition skills. Tutors might encourage students to bring in the lyrics from their favorite CDs, keeping in mind the qualifier that the lyrics must be appropriate for school reading activities—that is, no explicit sex, violence, racism, or "hate" lyrics. Reading of lyrics also tends to improve fluency, rhythm, and expression in oral reading as students already have a strong sense of these features from the songs. These readings are great to tape-record.
- Plays and scripts make excellent vehicles for reading together. Drama, including television and film scripts, is a wonderful resource for read-alouds and partner reading. The librarian or head of the English department is an excellent source for these scripts. Tutors will be surprised at just how much their students enjoy reading these and will find that they enjoy the script reading as much as their students do. These readings are also great to tape-record.
- Young Adult, or YA, fiction is a thriving sub-genre that includes books dealing with topical adolescent issues in language and format that are accessible to students being tutored. Librarians are a great source for ideas.

- Fiction includes novels and short stories. Of particular interest to students likely to be tutored are sub-genres, such as fantasy, horror, science fiction, adventure, suspense, mystery, and romance.
- Research shows that males generally prefer non-fiction reading materials. A wide range of non-fiction provides excellent sources for tutoring. Biographies and autobiographies of musicians, actors,

and athletes tend to be of special interest to students being tutored. Non-fiction also includes textbooks, newspapers, magazines, letters, e-mails, diaries or journals, manuals, interviews, and recipes.

- Magazines on specific topics of interest, such as sports, music, films, television programs, auto mechanics, and popular culture, also appeal to many students. If encouraged by their tutors, many students will bring in favorite magazines. In turn, tutors might look for recent or back issues of some of these magazines. Reading an issue of a favorite magazine is a gift to us all.
- Some tutors have used driver's manuals to advantage with older students.

"Genre Inventory" is an instrument useful for determining kinds of texts that individual students find interesting. A template appears as an appendix; a completed version appears here.

Genre Inventory

Name: _Gord_

Kinds of Books/Texts I Like to Read	A Lot	Somewhat	Not Much
1. Fiction			
a) fantasy	☐	☑	☐
b) horror	☑	☐	☐
c) science fiction	☐	☑	☐
d) adventure	☐	☐	☑
e) suspense	☑	☐	☐
f) mystery	☐	☑	☐
g) romance	☐	☐	☑
2. Non-Fiction			
a) biographies	☑	☐	☐
b) autobiographies	☐	☐	☑
c) textbooks	☐	☐	☑
d) newspapers	☐	☐	☑
e) magazines	☑	☐	☐
f) letters	☐	☐	☑
g) e-mails	☐	☑	☐
h) diaries/journals	☐	☐	☑
i) manuals	☐	☐	☑
j) interviews	☐	☐	☑
3. Poetry/Lyrics	☐	☑	☐
4. Drama	☐	☐	☑

According to a 2006 survey of tutors in semi-urban Ontario, Canada, there are interesting similarities and differences according to age groups in the topics that most interest dependent readers in tutoring situations (Berrill 2006).

Students in Grades 2 and 3	Students in Grades 7 to 10
1. Animals	1. Adventure
2. Humor	2. Humor
3. Family	3. Biography/Autobiography
4. Fairytales/Legends	4. Sport
5. Insects	5. Animals
6. Nature	6. History/Current Events
7. Sports	7. Suspense
8. Holidays/Seasons	8. Forensics
9. Adventure	9. Drama

The two groups shared four interest categories—adventure, humor, animals, and sports. Interestingly, humor was the second-most popular category for both young and older learners. The other categories were, as might be anticipated, quite different. Not surprisingly, younger learners expressed interest in family and fairytales or legends—things within their experiential realm—as well as insects, holidays, and seasons, which are part of everyday life in semi-urban settings. Older learners developed more interest in typically adolescent topics such as biographies or autobiographies—usually of popular personalities; sports; history, including current events; suspense; forensics (likely as a result of television); drama, including television and film scripts; and games, including computer games.

As learners become older, gender preferences for topics become more pronounced. When choosing texts, these preferences should be actively taken into account and students' diversity of interests kept in mind.

Boys in Grades 9 and 10	Girls in Grades 9 and 10
1. Adventure	1. Adventure
2. Humor	2. Biography
3. Sports	3. Humor
4. Animals	4. Historical
5. Biography	5. Forensics/Crime
6. Historical	6. Family
7. Games	7. Computers/Video
8. Current Events	8. Drama
9. Suspense	9. Food
10. Forensics/Crime	10. Sports

Boys and girls in Grades 9 and 10 often picked books with similar topics: adventure, humor, biography, sports, historical, and forensics/crime. Other favorite topics were more gender specific. The boys' list included some topics not rated highly by girls—these included animals, games, suspense, and current events. The girls chose books on such topics as computers/videos, drama, family, and food with greater frequency than boys.

Effective tutors check regularly with students to determine that the chosen texts match students' interests.

Although the topics selected will vary according to the gender, as well as the cultural and regional backgrounds, of the students being surveyed, it is the *diversity* of interests that tutors should keep in mind. If tutors are to activate the prior knowledge that is critical for effective decoding, fluency, and comprehension, they need to ensure that students are interested in and familiar with the topic of the text being read. Checking regularly with students to determine that the texts match their interests is essential.

"Interest Inventory," with a template on page 145, is an instrument that can be used to determine topics of interest to students. Teachers may have conducted a similar inventory before tutors arrive. If so, they should alert tutors to the specific preferences of the students they are tutoring. Otherwise, tutors could administer "Interest Inventory" as a good and quick diagnostic tool early in the tutoring program.

Interest Inventory

Name: *Liam*

Topics That Interest Me	A Lot	Somewhat	Not Much
Sports such as *Snowboarding*	☑	☐	☐
Animals such as *dogs, wolves*	☑	☐	☐
Humor	☑	☐	☐
Relationships (family/friends)	☐	☑	☐
Fantasy	☐	☑	☐
Music	☑	☐	☐
Visual Art	☐	☐	☑
Drama	☐	☐	☑
Dancing	☐	☐	☑
Biography/Autobiography about *athletes*	☑	☐	☐
Games	☐	☑	☐
Television Programs and Personalities	☐	☑	☐
Films	☐	☑	☐
Vehicles	☑	☐	☐
Nature/Outdoors	☑	☐	☐
The Environment	☐	☑	☐
Popular Culture	☐	☑	☐
Science	☐	☐	☑
History	☐	☐	☑
Romance	☐	☐	☑
Crafts/Hobbies *working on small engines*	☑	☐	☐
Computers/Technology	☑	☐	☐
War	☐	☑	☐
Health	☐	☐	☑

Pros and Cons of Levelled Texts

As teachers will know, educational publishers offer series of texts that include a range of individual titles written at different levels of difficulty. These texts have been levelled for both content and language, such as vocabulary and sentence structure. There are both advantages and disadvantages to using levelled texts in a tutoring program.

Often, dependent readers become frustrated due to trying to read books that are too difficult for them—an issue that levelled texts address. Access to a set of texts that are appropriate to the age of the student, written on a wide range of topics, and at a variety of levels of difficulty significantly increases the chances of matching the student to appropriate text. Selecting a text that meets the individual needs of the student improves the student's chances of success. This success motivates further reading. Teachers play an important role in directing tutors to these texts or to someone else, such as the librarian, who can locate these texts for tutor perusal.

Some care should be taken in the selection of levelled texts, however. Students may find them uninteresting. In an effort to reduce the complexity of the vocabulary and the sentence structure, publishers may have reduced the richness of literature. Students will soon let their tutors know if they sense that an author is talking down to them. Tutors will have to pay close attention to student reactions to a given text. With one that is failing to engage the student, they should be prepared to speed up the reading by sharing the task.

> Students can work with more difficult texts as long as their tutors recognize that these will require partner reading.

Use of Online Resources

Some students have previous negative experiences with printed texts, so they may respond more positively to online texts in a tutoring situation. Many tutors are delighted to make use of the Internet to find information on topics that interest their students. Teachers should alert tutors to this source of text material and advise them to preview any Web sites that will be accessed with the student before going online with the student. In turn, tutors should let teachers know about Web sites that are of particular interest to students. Given the interactive nature of the Internet, it may be particularly compelling for students to write a response to an Internet site. If so, tutors should save and print those responses, along with the original Web site information.

Kinds of online texts that tutors have found useful include celebrity Web sites, online newspapers and magazines, Web sites of favorite sports teams, reviews of current movies and television programs, Web sites of favorite authors, Web sites on topics of personal interest to the student, virtual museums, and Web sites with song lyrics. An appendix, "Web Sites with Information on Choosing Books for Young Adults," identifies specific sites that list books proven to appeal to young adults.

Recognize the Need for Engaging Resources

The challenge facing the tutor is how to match the student's needs and interests to an appropriate text. Informal discussions between the tutor and the student as well as more formal diagnostic tools, such as reading interest inventories, are critical to finding a good match.

The teacher is an invaluable source of information about student interests and abilities. By providing as much background as possible to the tutor, the teacher helps the tutor avoid wasted time and energy, especially early in the tutoring process.

Proper text selection is critical to increasing fluency and improving comprehension. If the student doesn't engage with the text, the likelihood of success is reduced significantly. Before selecting texts for tutoring, then, it is important to learn about the student's background and interests. As this chapter notes, the student's reading level, as well as the text's level of difficulty, source, kind, and topic, affect text selection.

Chapter 10 How to Promote Fluency and Word Recognition

Comprehension depends on reading at a fast enough speed to remember what has been read from the beginning of a sentence or paragraph. Skilled readers are able to accurately and quickly recognize words so that they can focus on making meaning as they read, rather than spending time with painstaking word-by-word decoding.

Two factors determine success at reading: fluency and automaticity. **Fluency** is the ability to read orally with accuracy, expression, and at a fast enough rate to be able to focus on making meaning rather than decoding (Griffith and Rasinski 2004). **Automaticity** is the ability of a reader to automatically and accurately recognize words. Automatic word recognition is necessary for fluency, for comprehension, and for sustained reading of more complex reading material.

Many dependent readers have difficulty reading quickly and accurately enough to comprehend the material. Their reading is halting and oftentimes jerky as they focus on decoding individual words. This focus takes valuable cognitive time, and by the time these readers identify individual words, they may well have forgotten the material that preceded those words. Automatic recognition of words is not all that is needed for comprehension, but it is a necessary component (Clark 2004).

It is generally agreed that by sixth grade, fluent readers typically read at an oral rate of 110 to 150 words per minute and at a silent rate of 160 to 190 words per minute. Teachers need to let tutors know that with students 11 years or older, there is a fluency problem if the student is reading aloud at a speed of anything less than 100 words per minute (wpm).

Speed, however, isn't everything when it comes to fluency: some students read incredibly fast, yet convey little emotion and expression while reading. They struggle to comprehend. Those students need to be encouraged to slow down, pay attention to punctuation, read with expression, and do the during-reading activities that will build their comprehension habits of mind.

In contrast to fluent readers, dependent readers read aloud at about the same speed as they read silently. The easiest way to time silent reading is to ask students to read something brand new to them for one minute. Students start at the top and continue on down, reading as they normally would. The timing begins as soon as they begin reading. Tutor or teacher should watch their eyes and body language and record any observations—eyes jumpy or not, seems to lose place, follows with finger. At one

We have named a different kind of fluency problem the Bernadette problem. One of us had a student named Bernadette who loved *Romeo and Juliet*. She always volunteered to read aloud and she read very fast. She sometimes made up variations of words or skipped words entirely. Her comprehension suffered and so did that of some of the listeners—Bernadette thought reading was just "saying the words on the page real fast, with some kind of expression."

Reminding tutors that some silent reading behaviors can be helpful is a good idea. The value of the behavior depends on what is being read, how often the student uses the behavior, and whether it works to improve comprehension. For example, it is helpful to skim an information text for one or two seconds before reading; however, skimming a lot while reading or flipping pages randomly does not increase comprehension. Similarly, stopping and rereading once or twice on a page can be very helpful; doing so five times would hinder comprehension of longer text.

minute, timers, likely tutors, gently ask readers to stop and place a finger on the last word read.

It is important to see if students have a basic understanding of what they read silently. Seasoned tutors first congratulate students on reading so much; then, ask students to tell them about what they read. They note where students ended reading and after the tutoring session, count the number of words read. They then ask students to read aloud the same piece and see how many words they read aloud in one minute. Students will likely read the passage better, as technically they are rereading. Older fluent readers will read silently about one-third faster than they read aloud.

Adopting a checklist, such as the example, will help determine what work a student needs to do on fluency. Tutors may administer it, using either a watch with a second hand or the clock on the wall.

The behaviors noted in the checklist are usually not obvious. In the classroom context, there is probably not enough time to monitor older students' reading fluency in this way. Encouraging tutors to use this checklist provides teachers with information that they can use to inform their own teaching practices. If teachers are alerted by tutors to problems, they may wish to administer the checklist in timed reading themselves, to corroborate tutor findings. A template of the "Fluency Checklist" appears as an appendix.

Fluency Checklist

Name: _Zac_   Date: _October 4, 2006_

Length of passage: _200 words_

Silent reading time: _2_ minutes and _23_ seconds

Oral reading time: _2_ minutes and _30_ seconds

When reading aloud, does the student	Rarely	Sometimes	Often
• stop frequently?	☑	☐	☐
• make inappropriate pauses?	☐	☑	☐
• read word by word?	☐	☐	☑
• speak in flat, monotone voice?	☐	☐	☑
• miss emotional and contextual cues?	☐	☐	☑
• mix up who says which piece of dialogue in a narrative?	☐	☑	☐
• pay little attention to punctuation?	☐	☑	☐
• painstakingly sound out words?	☑	☐	☐
• have difficulty with sounds?	☑	☐	☐
• fail to recognize recurring words?	☑	☐	☐
• emphasize the wrong syllable?	☑	☐	☐
• ignore suffixes and prefixes?	☑	☐	☐
When reading silently, does the student			
• read at about the same speed as when reading aloud?	☐	☐	☑
• shift eyes often on the page?	☑	☐	☐
• need to stop and reread often?	☑	☐	☐
• seem to skim large chunks of text?	☑	☐	☐

Comments and next steps: Zac needs to work on hearing the emotion in what he reads and pay attention to punctuation. We will use easy texts, modelled expressive reading, emphasis and intonation, and taped readings

Zac has great word recognition skills. He tends to get the words right, but doesn't have expression or meaning in his voice; consequently, he struggles to understand what he is reading. We will do more work on during-reading strategies [see Chapter 7] in addition to fluency

Fluency issues don't disappear over night, but do get better over time. If tutors complete fluency checklists monthly and share results with their students, both tutors and students will see progress.

If a student gets a Sometimes or Often on many of the questions in the "Fluency Checklist," that student needs the following strategies: easy texts, modelled expressive reading, Readers Theatre, emphasis and intonation, taped oral readings, and additional timed readings. These are outlined in the pages that follow.

Providing Easy Texts

Students need to read as many texts at their independent (easy) reading level as time allows. Doing so will increase their accuracy and reading rate as well as their confidence. Students need to know what fluent reading feels like and sounds like: this knowledge will help them recognize when they are having difficulty. They need to experience the ease of reading to build stamina for reading texts at their instructional level.

Modelling Expressive Reading

Students will benefit when tutors model expressive reading—show pizzazz when they read aloud. The most effective read-alouds to students have some common characteristics (Fisher et al. 2004). Tutor-modelled read-alouds occur in a variety of forms, from partner reading to straightforward reading aloud to students. For instance, tutors might read passages to their students and then ask them to read it with them orally in unison.

- Texts match learner interests and connect with them emotionally.
- Tutors preview and practise readings before presenting.
- Tutors read fluently with few, if any, pronunciation errors. Their voices are animated and expressive. They serve as models.
- Tutors stop periodically and ask questions based on what is contributing to the fluency. For example: "How did I know to get angry when I read, 'What are you doing here?'"

Doing Readers Theatre

Most tutors will be unfamiliar with Readers Theatre, so teachers need to suggest this strategy to them.

Readers Theatre is interpretative oral reading. All of the meaning and emotion in a passage is evoked through voices, as if the readers are on the radio. There are no costumes, props, movement, or gestures. In Readers Theatre, the readers have practised reading a text expressively many times before reading it aloud to an audience.

Students who struggle with fluency need this kind of activity *most* (Griffith and Rasinski 2004). They need to hear the voices behind the words so that the words come alive. Poems, monologues, writing for two voices—these all make words jump off the page and are perfect for Readers Theatre. The tutor and the student can practise a text together and perform it for an adult, friend, family member, teacher, or other student and tutor pair. Or the reading can be audiotaped and listened to repeatedly at later dates. It is a good idea to begin all audiotapes by noting, "This is

See "Books to Help Develop Fluency," on page 151, for a list of potential books for Readers Theatre and expressive reading. Any texts that students enjoy reading should also be considered.

Many picture books are great for Readers Theatre because they have eloquent character voices and deal with contemporary issues. In addition, because of the detailed visuals and lower word count, they are more accessible for dependent readers. Librarians are excellent resources for identifying books that are particularly compelling.

[name of student]. Today's date is _____ and I am going to read _____."

Enterprising tutors can also create a Readers Theatre poem or script from any informational text by pulling out some key words and adding a few phrases. In time, students and tutors can create Readers Theatre scripts together. This great writing activity should take only 10 minutes or even less if students have a strong musical intelligence and if they like to rap. To do this, tutors and students randomly choose interesting words from a text and then say them both alternately and periodically together.

For example, from an informational text on teen budgeting, a Readers Theatre poem for two voices can be created:

Reader 1: dating
Reader 2: entertainment
R1 and 2: take a big chunk out of your wallet
R1: do the math
R2: and KISS
R1 and 2: Keep It Simple, Smart guy
R1: don't spend a mint
R2: spend a minute and think
R1: cook dinner at home and
R2: go out for dessert
R1: order appetizers
R2: not the entrée
R1: sip water with icy lemon
R2: not pop
R1: hold on
R2: hold on
R1 and R2: hold on to your money because one day it might be gone

Exploring Emphasis and Intonation

Emphasis is everything in a sentence. The meaning of a sentence depends on which words are emphasized. One exercise that teachers might introduce tutors to involves asking students to say the same sentence in three or four different ways: students will see how meaning shifts based on intonation. For example:

I liked that movie.
I *liked* that movie.
I liked *that* movie.
I liked that *movie*.

Tutors would then engage students in discussing how the meaning shifts as the emphasis shifts.

Tutor: When might you emphasize "I" in this sentence?
Student: When other people didn't like it.
Tutor: Right! And when might you emphasize "that"?
Student: I guess when other people liked a different one.

Tutor: Exactly. So, it's not just the words in a sentence that matter. How we emphasize individual words also matters because the emphasis can change the meaning.

Tutors might also ask students to change the punctuation marks and say the same sentence aloud. Consider these variations:

You like her.
You like her!
You like her?

After discussing punctuation marks, tutors can ask students to create a sentence, change the word that gets stressed, and discuss how the meaning changes based on the emphasis, or students can change the punctuation and discuss how the meaning changes based on the punctuation.

Taping Oral Readings

A good idea is for tutors to tape students reading aloud for one minute. The tapings should be done near the start of the tutoring program and at periodic tutoring sessions after that, with the date given at the beginning of each reading. Tapings allow listeners to hear progress over time.

As mentioned earlier, whenever taping is done, students need to identify themselves, the date, and the passage they are reading. Not only will they be better able to compare their own readings and hear their progress, but the classroom teacher can also listen to the readings, reinforce progress, and make suggestions to tutors. The teacher might also want to listen to the tapes alone at a later time in light of the "Fluency Checklist" to discover if students' fluency is improving.

Audiotapings also provide an audience for Readers Theatre and monologue reading. After doing several tapings, the student may wish to share the taped readings with others. Hearing themselves read, students become proud of the tapings and more confident too.

Teachers are responsible for introducing the idea of audiotaped oral readings to tutors and for providing the tape recorder and audiocassette.

Timing One-Minute Readings

Tutors may be asked to keep dated records on how many words students can read aloud expressively with appropriate phrasing and intonation in one minute. (See the sample next page.) As always, it is important to use engaging texts at the student's independent level, such as monologues, Readers Theatre scripts, poems, fascinating facts, and strange-but-true stories. As the student progresses, independent level texts should increase in difficulty.

In creating a table of readings, it is important that reading level and type of text are considered—any comparisons should be made between similar texts. For instance, all passages might be from a history textbook or they might be stories. There is a real difference between reading aloud a page from a textbook and reading aloud a teen story. Encouraging stu-

Even just taping students reading aloud the same text at the beginning of the tutoring and at the end of tutoring enables students to *hear* the difference in their own reading. This tangible evidence of improvement is extremely rewarding and motivating for them.

dents to reread a section is recommended because they will see that they can increase their speed with rereading.

Showing students their progress on a table become a powerful motivational device. The table can also be used to construct a bar graph, showing increase in number of words over time.

Date	Title of Text	# of words read in 1 minute with expression, phrasing, and intonation
Sept 26	Should Uniforms Be Mandatory in School?	88 (little expression)
Oct 10	Amazing Amazons	88 (some expression)
Nov 14	Rats: The Facts	92 (some expression)
Nov 16	Rats: The Facts, second reading	96 (some expression)

Predicting Words and Ideas

We know that independent readers subconsciously scan a new text and predict what it will be about. Making a prediction calls for activating prior knowledge, including specific words associated with the topic. This habit of mind must be taught explicitly to dependent readers.

If properly guided, tutors can help students learn how to scan text and predict content and upcoming words when they first pick up a text. If students learn how to do this, they will be more likely to recognize upcoming words, rather than feel that words are coming at them "out of the blue." For example, the tutor asks, "What kinds of ideas are likely to come up in an article about teens loitering at malls?" The student then brainstorms five words likely to be in the text and explains why. To adapt this strategy, the tutor could ask the student to create an oral story that incorporates those five words. This discussion activates prior knowledge in the learner and usually leads to the student speaking aloud some of the words about to be read.

As well as being helpful for the specific text, this tutoring strategy underscores for dependent readers that word choice has a logic and that they can figure the logic out before they begin to read, anticipating the words and ideas they have predicted. This activity can become a game and, again, results can be recorded to note the increase in accuracy of the student's predictions.

The following strategies, from Chapter 7, also help build fluency: echo reading, repeated reading, partner reading, reading in unison, and reading to each other.

Strategies That Support Word Recognition

One of the key ways to increase fluency is to strengthen a student's word recognition skills. Word recognition is a broad category containing decoding (letter–sound recognition) and phonemic awareness; recognizing roots and affixes; recognizing sight words; recognizing small words in big words; and using structural context.

Before tutors can teach word recognition strategies, they need to be aware of the techniques that independent readers have internalized. They need to know some basic definitions, including those below. (See "Terms for Tutors," pages 12–13, which could be handed out to volunteers.)

- **Phonemes** are the smallest units of sound in a language that are represented by letters or combinations of letters. For example, the word "little" has four phonemes (/l/, /i/, /t/, /l/). The diagonal marks indicate the *sounds* rather than the letters
- **Graphemes** are graphic representations that represent the sounds: in western languages, these letters or letter combinations represent sounds. For example, the word "little" has six letters, but only four sounds [*litl*]. Note that the same word may have a different number of graphemes and phonemes.
- **Morphemes** are the smallest meaningful parts of words. They include prefixes, suffixes, and root words. Sample prefixes: un-; re-; im-. Sample suffixes: -ed; -ing; -er. Sample root word: *read*. Combinations include *reread, reader,* and *reading.*
- **Rimes** are vowels and any consonants that follow them in a syllable. In *hit, -it* is the rime and in *drool, -ool* is the rime.
- **Onsets** are the consonants prior to vowels. In *hit, h* is the onset and in *drool, dr* is the onset. Sometimes, rimes are called "word families." (Examples: *hit, bit, sit* or *drool, pool, fool*)

Reviewing Decoding Skills and Phonemic Awareness

A surprising number of adolescent dependent readers benefit from reviewing decoding skills and phonemic awareness. The following strategies for tutors help determine and build upon student awareness of sounds and letters, including short vowels, long vowels, consonants, digraphs (two letters representing one sound), and consonant blends.

Letter–Sound Recognition and Recall

Teachers may wish to alert tutors to the fact that even older students may have trouble with letter–sound recognition and benefit from practice in letter–sound recognition and recall.

A straightforward approach that even novice tutors can use is the following. The tutor makes up a sheet of paper with letters that seem to be problematic for the student. For instance, a student may be saying the /n/ sound for the letter "m." A short list would include the letters "n" and "m" plus several others that the student might already know. The tutor then asks the student, "Which letter makes the ___ sound?" The student makes the appropriate sound (phoneme). For the reverse activity, letter–sound recall, the tutor points to the relevant letter, for example, *t*, and asks the student, "What sound does this letter make?"

Since some letters make more than one sound, all correct answers should be acknowledged and tutors prompted to prod for additional sounds the letter makes. If students can easily identify sounds and letters, but still tend to use an incorrect sound for any letters during read-alouds, tutors would note the words where the difficulty is occurring and list them for practice in pronunciation.

The same activity can be done with **common blends**, where two consonants blend their sounds and the original sounds are still heard (e.g., /br/,

Students may be experiencing information-processing difficulties or may be learning English as an additional language. In either case, practice with individual letters and then with words helps them internalize conventional pronunciation.

/bl/, /sk/, /tr/), and **digraphs**, where two or more letters form a single new sound (e.g., /sch/, /ch/, /gh/, /th/, /ph/).

The tutor lists the blends or digraphs that cause the student difficulty. With the student, these are put on flash cards (or a list in the student's reading log) and the sounds practised with the student until they become automatic. The tutor can quiz the student and the student can also quiz the tutor.

Here are some options for practice:

- Games such as Go Fish using cards with the letter combinations make practice fun.
- Tutors may find words that contain these letter combinations in real reading that students want to do and practise those words.
- Students may create flash cards and use the words orally in their own dialogue or Readers Theatre scripts.

Phonemic Awareness

Through read-alouds or conversation, tutors may notice that students are mispronouncing words or excluding letters. This may be true for someone with an undiagnosed information-processing need or for someone learning English as an additional language. Regardless, the student needs to reinforce how to distinguish different sounds and practise making sounds.

The tutor makes a list of words and asks the student to say each word once and then repeat it with a change indicated by the tutor. At the beginning, the tutor should use compound words, but as they continue, just use words that can have a sound removed and still be words.

For example, the tutor begins by saying, "Say the word 'butterfly'" and the student responds, "Butterfly." Then the tutor says, "Now, say it again, but don't say *butter*" and the student says, "fly." Then the tutor says, "Say the word 'snowman'" and then, "Now, say it again, but don't say *man*." Next, the tutor says, "Say the word 'boat'" and then, "Now, say it again, but don't say /b/." This activity can continue with the tutor eliminating the sound of the initial consonant in a word, the final consonant in a word, the initial consonant in a consonant blend (e.g., "freak" and "Say it again but don't say /f/.") and the second consonant in a consonant blend (e.g., "slip" and "'Say it again, but don't say /l/."). These are adaptations of the Rosner Test of Auditory Skills to determine a student's phonemic awareness. It is a good idea to encourage the student to generate words with a sound removed to try to stump the tutor.

Teach Rime Patterns

Teachers need to let tutors know that students are empowered when they can talk about and then identify language features, using appropriate terminology. It is important to teach the correct terminology: *onset* as the beginning part of the word; *rime* as the ending part. Tutors can reinforce that a rime is what allows a word to rhyme.

To do this, the tutor makes a list of words using the rime needing practice (e.g., *-ush* as in *blush, crush, flush, rush, hush*) and asks the student to explain what is the same and what is different in each word. The tutor might also prompt the student to make up other words with the same rime.

Experienced tutors will learn to keep lists of words with the same pattern in students' notes and use them in Readers Theatre scripts and jointly created writing. From time to time, they review the list, add to it, and reinforce the patterns through more practice.

Working with Prefixes, Suffixes, and Root Words

Tutors and learners can play a variety of games to help the learners gain a better understanding of prefixes, suffixes, and root words, something that will allow them to make better sense of text.

Word Search Puzzles

A **word search puzzle** is a grid full of letters where the student looks for words at different angles, and circles or highlights them. Words might be written from left to right, top to bottom, or from right to left and bottom to top. They might also be written on the diagonal.

Word search puzzles help reinforce spelling patterns. They can be used to reinforce word families, consonant blends and digraphs, or prefixes, suffixes, and root words. Word searches might be used when words or morphemes are introduced. Similarly, once tutors identify the errors that students make with prefixes, suffixes, and root words as they read, they may develop word search puzzles based on those words. For example, the word search might feature words with the prefix *un-*, as in *unsatisfied*, *unmotivated*, *unattractive*, *unnecessary*, and *unusual*.

A word search puzzle is easy to create. There are many free online programs that can create puzzles in seconds, for example, Discovery School's tool at http://puzzlemaker .school.discovery.com. The word search below was generated at that Web site.

Word Search for the Prefix *un-*

U	G	R	N	I	Q	N	Y	O	U	H	K
T	N	Y	I	H	D	D	D	F	N	P	T
V	M	S	T	J	V	N	L	J	M	L	I
Y	Z	A	A	Y	U	H	S	C	O	C	Y
P	P	B	L	T	M	O	O	F	T	K	L
M	P	P	Q	A	I	H	I	C	I	Y	A
W	Y	N	A	X	D	S	O	M	V	Z	U
M	H	I	N	H	W	E	F	U	A	Y	S
Q	F	T	B	L	N	Q	H	I	T	I	U
G	O	V	Z	U	V	U	T	J	E	F	N
Y	F	T	A	Q	Z	I	D	F	D	D	U
Y	R	A	S	S	E	C	E	N	N	U	V

Words to find:

UNDO

UNMOTIVATED

UNSATISFIED

UNHAPPY

UNNECESSARY

UNUSUAL

Word Construction

To strengthen word recognition, tutors may print a series of prefixes written on file cards (e.g., *un-, pre-, re-, un-, mal-, dis-, co-*) and, on separate cards, a series of words that can be combined with the prefixes (e.g., *happy, read, usual, content, agree, operate, zip*). The second set of cards should be in a different color from the prefix cards. Students can then practise putting the prefixes together with the words (e.g., *unhappy*) and through moving the cards, come to recognize how the meaning of a word changes when a prefix is added. The same approach can be taken with suffixes (e.g., *-ed, -er, -est, -able, -ist, -ing, -ly, -ful*) with changes in meaning noted.

These exercises help students generate rules about what happens when certain prefixes or suffixes are added to words. For instance, the student might make the words "unhappy," "unusual," and "unzip." The tutor would ask the student to define each word and then provide a meaning for the prefix. The tutor–student dialogue below provides an example of how the definition of a prefix is generated.

It is important to reinforce prefix and suffix definitions in future readings to help students internalize their meanings and understand unknown words.

Tutor: I'd like you to combine one of these prefixes with each of these three words. First, please read the words for me.
Student: Happy, usual, and zip.
Tutor: Great. Now which of these three prefixes would sound right with all three of those words?
Student: Uhmmm. Let's see. *Dis* … no, *dishappy* isn't a word.
Tutor: You're right. It's not.
Student: Uhmm. I think *un* would work.
Tutor: Let's try it.
Student: Well, there's *unhappy*. That works. And *unusual*. That's a word too.
Tutor: Good for you! What about *zip*?
Student: Sure. *Unzip*!
Tutor: Way to go! Now, let's define each word. What does *unhappy* mean?
Student: Not happy.
Tutor: Right! And *unusual*?
Student: Not usual?
Tutor: That's right. What does that mean, *not usual*?
Student: Well … it means it doesn't usually happen.
Tutor: Yes?
Student: Well, not often.
Tutor: Okay! And *unzip*?
Student: That's easy! Undo!
Tutor: Look! You've come up with another one! *Undo*!
Student: Yeah. Pretty good!
Tutor: You sure are. So, what do you think *un* means?
Student: Uhmm … the opposite.
Tutor: Yes, that's true. But we don't say "opposite happy."
Student: (*laughing*) That's weird.
Tutor: (*laughing*) It is. What's a different word we might use?
Student: Uhmm…. Maybe *not*?
Tutor: Let's try it and see if it works.

Teach the Meaning of Word Parts

Once tutors have information about common prefixes, suffixes, and roots, they can help students learn more about how words work by combining prefixes and suffixes with root words. It is often helpful to begin with a few common prefixes and suffixes and have students memorize these. The morphemes can be written on file cards with the definition of each written on a different card. A game similar to Go Fish can be played where one person asks the other person either for a given definition or for the morpheme. For example, tutors holding the prefix *dis-* might ask, "Do you have the word 'not'?" Or students with the word "under" might ask, "Do you have the prefix *sub-*?" The person with the greatest number of pairs wins. As well, student and tutor can play a game where they try to think of as many words as possible with a given prefix or suffix.

Some Common Morphemes

Prefixes		Suffixes	
bi-, di-	two (*bicycle, divide*)	-er	more; person who does something (*bigger, painter*)
con-, com-	with, together (*conversation*)	-est	most (*biggest*)
dis-	away, not (*disagree*)	-ful	having a particular quality; full of (*hopeful*)
mis-	bad, badly (*misinform*)	-ish	like something; having a particular quality (*foolish*)
non-	not (*nonsense*)	-ist	person who studies or practises something (*artist*)
pre-	before (*predict*)		
re-	again; back (*reread*)	-less	without (*careless, homeless*)
sub-	under; below (*submarine*)	-ly	in a certain way; changes an adjective into an adverb (*sadly, quickly*)
tri-	three (*tripod*)		
un-	not (*unhappy*)	-ness	state of being; changes an adjective (descriptive word) into a noun (*happiness*)
		-tion	changes a verb into a noun (*connection, formation*)

Make a Suffix Chart

Tutor–student teams could make four-column suffix charts, much like that shown below. They might work on a computer screen or on large paper.

Root Word	-er	-est	-ly
quick	quicker	quickest	quickly
slow	slower	slowest	slowly
strong	stronger	strongest	strongly

Tutors prompt their students to add appropriate suffixes to each root word and fill in the grid with the new words. They discuss the words that can be made by adding the suffix and how the words—and meanings—change as a result. Together, they note any new words that do not make sense.

Increasing Students' Sight Word Banks

Students need to have an extensive bank of **sight words**, or words they recognize instantly, in order to read fluently. Tutors can help dependent readers develop this.

Using Word Lists

Depending on students' reading levels, teachers may provide tutors with the traditional lists of high-frequency words, such as the Dolch Sight Word List, designed for children reading at Kindergarten through Grade 3 level, or the Frye Instant Word List. These lists may be used to diagnostically assess how many words their students can instantly recognize.

Students need to experience success, so it is best for tutors to begin with the first 100 words and work up from there. When a student begins having difficulty, the tutor should note the tricky word, write it on a flash card, and bring it to a subsequent tutoring session. Depending on the student's fatigue level, the tutor does not stop at the first tricky word, only after the student misses 5 to 10 words.

Tutors should date this assessment and do another assessment of sight words at the end of the tutoring program. They can then compare the number of words known at the beginning and at the end of the tutoring. This comparison becomes tangible evidence to students of their progress and is highly motivating to them.

This activity can get tiresome, so it's important to keep it short and fresh. One way to add spice is to have tutors create flash cards from 4 by 6 file cards that show high-frequency words from the students' own reading; for example, if a student likes reading about forensics, perhaps the words "autopsy," "cadaver," and "skeletal" could be written on flash cards.

Recognizing Words Within Large Words

Dependent readers benefit from learning how words, as units of meaning, combine to form compound words or become embedded in complex words. Tutors can help them make better meaning of large words.

Explore Compound Words

When advisable, tutors may explore compound words with their learners. On a theme or topic that interests their students, they make a list of compound words related to the theme. Whenever possible, it is preferable to involve students in creating lists like this. For example, for someone interested in winter sports, compound words could focus on the word "snow" (e.g., *snowboard, snowmobile, snowflake, snowpants*). Tutors put the words that make up the compound words on separate cards. They then have the students say various new combinations of words aloud.

Think Aloud About Word Chunks

When they come across a new word, independent readers break it down into smaller, recognizable chunks. Tutors can helpfully model this strategy. For example, the tutor could say: "When I see an unknown word, like 'metallurgist,' I notice that it starts with *metal* and that makes me think of steel and gold. I'm not sure what *-urgist* means, but I see another small part of the word that I do know—*ist*. I think words that end in *-ist* tend to be nouns—like dentist and scientist. So, this could be a person who works with metals. Let's look it up in the dictionary and see how close I am."

Using Structural Context

Dependent readers will recognize new words faster if they can recognize the parts of speech that the words should be. This knowledge is part of the syntactic cueing system (see Chapter 1) and should be explicitly taught to students whenever possible. If an unknown word comes after the word "the," then the unknown word is likely a noun. That provides a starting point for meaning. Explicit modelling will help dependent readers learn to make good guesses at unknown words.

Tutors can show students how to use word position to help determine meaning and can review parts of speech. For example, if tutors have file cards, they might write one adjective on each card. They would write a few sentences on chart paper, leaving most of the adjectives out of the sentences. They would then ask their students: "Where would you put the adjective? How do you know that?"

This activity can be modified with a focus on nouns, verbs, or pronouns. Great storybooks by Ruth Heller can also be used for teaching parts of speech. These titles include *Many Luscious Lollypops: A Book About Adjectives*, *A Cache of Jewels and Other Collective Nouns*, and *Mine, All Mine: A Book About Pronouns*. Finally, *Mad-libs*, which allow students to create stories by substituting various parts of speech, are available online. They provide many fun activities. Once students have a sense of these, it is possible to write them quite quickly as one of several activities within a tutoring session.

Making a Difference

Tutors can make a tremendous difference in the lives of their students. With fluent reading, students begin to hear the words on a page speak to them. Now the words carry relevance. Now the words are alive—inspiring, provoking, shocking, and entertaining. Now students can experience the joy of reading, some kind of emotional experience that changes them. Fluency is a crucial component of successful reading: without it, words are just words, carrying no meaning.

It is fluency—hearing words come alive—that enabled Martin Luther King Jr. to lift people up when he told them of his dream. Increasing students' fluency is giving them the keys to the kingdom.

Appendixes

Ladle Rat Rotten Hut: A Translation

This teacher resource can be used to help prospective tutors appreciate the challenges that less skilled readers face when trying to understand text. The story "Ladle Rat Rotten Hut" appears without the translation in Chapter 2 of *Tutoring Adolescent Readers*, where a possible training session is outlined.

Wants pawn term, dare worsted ladle gull hoe lift witter murder inner ladle cordage honour itch offer louge, dock florist. Disc ladle gull orphan worry putty ladle rat hut, end for disc raisin pimple caulder Ladle Rat Rotten Hut.

Once upon a time, there was a little girl who lived with her mother in a little cottage on the edge of a large, dark forest. This little girl often wore a pretty little red hood, and for this reason, people called her Little Red Riding Hood.

Wan mourning Rat Rotten Hut's murder colder inset: "Ladle Rat Rotten Hut, heresy ladle basking insome burden barter and shirker cockles. Tisk disc ladle basking tudor cordage offer groin murder hoe lifts honour udder site offer florist. Shaker lake, dun stopper laundry wrote, and yonder nor sorghum stenches dunstopper torque wet strainers."

One morning, Red Riding Hood's mother called her inside. "Little Red Riding Hood, here is a little basket and some bread and butter and sugar cookies. Take this little basket to the cottage of your grandmother who lives on the other side of the forest. Shake a leg, don't stop along the road, and under no circumstances, don't stop to talk with strangers."

"Hoe-cake, Murder," resplendent Ladle Rat Rotten Hut, an tickle ladle basking on stuttered oft. Honour wrote tudor cordage offer groin murder, Ladle Rat Rotten Hut mitten a bag woof.

"Okay, Mother," responded Little Red Riding Hood, and took the little basket and started off. On the road to the cottage of her grandmother, Little Red Riding Hood met a big wolf.

"Wail, wail, wail," set disc wicket woof, "evanescent Ladle Rat Rotten Hut! Wares or putty ladle gull goring wizard ladel basking?"

"Well, well, well," said this wicked wolf, "if it isn't Little Red Riding Hood! Where is our pretty little girl going with her little basket?"

"Armor goring tumor groin murder's," reprisal ladle gull. "Grammar's seeking bet. Armor ticking arson burden barter and sirker cockles."

"I'm going to my grandmother's," replied the little girl. "Grandma's sick in bed. I'm taking her some bread and butter and sugar cookies."

"Will, heifer blessing woke," setter wicket woof, butter taught tomb shelf: "Oil tickle shirt court tudor cordage offer groin murder. Oil ketchup wetter letter on. Den … heh heh heh!"

"Well, have a pleasant walk," said the wicked wolf, but he thought to himself, "I'll take a short cut to the cottage of her grandmother. I'll catch up with her later on. Then … heh, heh, heh!"

MURAL: Yonder nor sorghum stenches shut ladle gulls stopper torque wet strainers!

Moral: Under no circumstances should little girls stop to talk with strangers!

Modified from the original, found in *Anguish Languish* by Howard L. Chace (Prentice Hall, 1956)

Strategies for Tutoring Kinesthetic Learners

Kinesthetic learners learn best by taking a hands-on approach and actively exploring the physical world around them. Below are selected strategies that support kinesthetic learners in a tutoring situation.

Before-Reading Strategies

- Go for a brisk walk around the halls or the playground before settling into work.
- Invite the learner to look at all the pictures in a book in order to get an idea of the book's content.
  - Prompt the reader to tell you what the text is about.
- If the school has them, use letter tiles or letter dice to have the learner construct words that are in the text.
- Use word games that call for physical activity, such as beanbag toss.
  - For instance, place word cards on the floor. The learner tosses the beanbag onto a card and reads that card.
- Select reading materials on topics that interest the student. You may be able to refer to a survey that the student has completed.
- Have the student create a graphic organizer about a new text, either by hand or by using a computer. For instance, the student might create a mind map about skateboarding, placing the word "skateboarding" in a circle in the middle of the page and drawing lines from that circle to other circles created around the page. In each of these other circles, the student will write the names of different things associated with skateboarding, such as equipment, types of jumps, and ramps. This activity would be done before any reading about skateboarding begins: prompted to think about what he or she already knows, the student is helped in being able to predict what the text might be about.

During-Reading Strategies

- Chunk the reading into manageable bits. Depending on the difficulty of the text, a chunk might be as short as one paragraph. After reading a paragraph, there would be a pause and brief conversation about what has just been read.
- Allow for frequent breaks.
  - Recognize that the student may frequently fidget and move about; incorporate the need to move in planning the activities for each tutoring session.
  - Sitting for long periods of time should be avoided. For example, in a 45-minute tutoring session, the activity should change at least every 15 minutes, with student movement, such as standing and stretching, planned for the break or for the next activity, perhaps writing on the board.
  - Allow the student to read in a standing position.
- Keep in mind that some kinesthetic learners find their reading fluency increases if they rotate their arm in a circular motion while reading.
- Invite the student to walk around with the book when reading.
- Provide a "stress ball" for the student to use while reading or listening.
- Have the student write on a chalkboard, easel, or computer screen when reviewing vocabulary.
- Do partner reading, taking turns reading from the text.
- Read parts of the text together, in unison.
- Have the student fill in a graphic organizer while reading the text, either manually or on the computer.

Strategies for Tutoring Kinesthetic Learners (continued)

After-Reading Strategies

- Play charades to quiz each other on parts of the book or to build vocabulary.

- Prepare index or cue cards with bits of information from a recently read text. Have the student arrange them in the proper sequence.

- Together, create a mural that illustrates a story's development.

- Have the student draw an event or idea of importance from the text.

- Invite the student to create a Wanted or Missing poster for a person, place, or thing from the story, either by hand or with a computer.

- Have the student act out a role in the text and then interview the student still as that character.

- Use games that provide opportunities for review and success.
  - For example, Grab Bag involves putting cards into a bag and having the student pull them out and respond. The cards might provide comprehension questions, sequence review, or vocabulary review.

- Prompt the student to complete an anticipation guide or graphic organizer for the text being read. The student may do it by hand or with a computer.

Strategies for Tutoring Students for Whom English Is a Second or Additional Language

Students who are learning English as a second or additional language bring a wealth of cultural experience with them. Tutors become cultural brokers with these students, helping them understand North American culture and also learning about their students' home cultures.

Before-Reading Strategies

- When possible, select texts on topics familiar to the students. Students can thereby focus on language building rather than on concept development.
- If learners have difficulty with understanding the sounds that make up the letters and words in the English language—that is, with phonemic awareness—use an activity or game that provides practice in the phonemic patterns that they find challenging. Examples: letter recognition, short and long vowels, consonants, digraphs (/th/, /ph/, /gh/), blends (/bl/, /gr/, /nd/), and word families (*hair, stair, pair*)
- If students have difficulty understanding parts of words, such as common prefixes, suffixes, and roots, use an activity or game that encourages them to combine parts of words in different ways for different meanings (*button, unbutton, buttoned*). For instance, students might combine prefix cards with root word cards to form new words. Doing so will improve their morphemic awareness.
- If students have a limited repertoire of English vocabulary, put new words on flash cards.
  - Keep the flash cards on a key ring or in a personal word box.
  - Have students practise defining the words before reading or have them teach what the words would be in their first language. Tutor and tutored can then quiz each other.
- Pre-teach vocabulary using some of the above strategies.
- Choose texts related to students' prior experiences and have students predict words or phrases that might be in the text.
- Bring in materials that support the text and discuss them with the student. For instance, if a student is reading *The Lord of the Rings*, you might bring in a piece of pita bread and ask the student to compare it with elfin bread.
- Have students create graphic organizers about new texts, either by hand or with a computer. For instance, if reading a history text about the First World War, students might create a t-chart with the headings Allies and Axis at the top. As they read, they could write down the names of Allied and Axis countries under the appropriate heading.

During-Reading Strategies

- Repeat readings of favorite passages to build fluency.
- Use the *cloze technique*: To prepare, type a passage of 50 to 100 words from the text, leaving a blank for every tenth word. When the student comes to a blank, ask for a word to fill it in. This exercise might be used as a quick review, immediately after the reading of the passage, before going on to the next part of the text.
- Use taped books or tape-record a text ahead of time. Let students be in charge of the tape recorder as they read along with the tape.
- Model reading for students, using talk-aloud protocols to explain the types of cueing systems and strategies that you are using to make sense of the text.

- Chunk the reading into manageable bits. With a difficult text, the chunk might be only a single paragraph long. You could follow the reading with an activity to help the student make meaning of the passage just read as well as the larger text. For instance, if focused on country alignments in the Second World War, it would be appropriate to pause after each paragraph to write on a t-chart the names of any new countries mentioned.

- Do partner reading, where tutor and tutored take turns reading the text, and also read the text in unison to build fluency and comprehension.

After-Reading Strategies

- Review sounds and words that students found difficult to pronounce while reading.

- Have students add new words and their definitions to their personal dictionaries.

- Encourage students to make picture dictionaries to illustrate word meanings.

- Encourage students to use their own words to outline main events or ideas from the text.

- Use graphic organizers and sequencing to reinforce comprehension. Students may do this either manually or with a computer.

- Together, identify cultural knowledge that is new either to you or the student and discuss similarities and differences in relation to the students' first language culture.

Strategies for Tutoring Students with Learning Disabilities

Challenges from learning disabilities come on a spectrum: some students are mildly affected, others significantly affected. Students with significant disability usually have an educational assistant working with them. Those facing fewer challenges usually will not. That said, any student who is identified by the school as having a learning disability will have an individual education plan: this plan identifies student strengths, needs, and strategies that might be used or tried.

As a tutor, you cannot have access to this documentation. The classroom teacher, though, can provide specific information on strategies that have been recommended for the student. Be sure to find out from the teacher if any teaching and learning strategies have been recommended.

Before-Reading Strategies

- Prepare a visual display which shows the connections between key terms and concepts presented in a text.
- Activate prior knowledge. Have students tell what they already know about the topic before beginning to read.
  - Together, jot these ideas down in point form or create a mind map.
- Use a graphic organizer to show how the main structural elements, such as characters, events, setting, conflicts, and resolutions, are related. For instance, in preparation for tutoring a student in a content area, the tutor might create a sequence map to show the events in mountain precipitation. The tutor and student would discuss this as an introduction to the concepts of mountain precipitation about to be presented in the text passage.
- Ask students to make predictions about what they are about to read or to create anticipation guides.
- Before beginning, set a clear purpose for reading. Sometimes, the purpose will be related to content of the passage. At other times, the purpose for reading might be to practise a certain strategy, such as using pragmatic cues to determine aspects of greater and lesser importance in the text.
- Pre-teach new or challenging vocabulary. Always begin by identifying the vocabulary to be addressed; then, choose the strategy to be used. The variety of strategies ranges from making words out of root words by adding prefixes and suffixes to having students create new entries for their personal dictionaries.
- Work with students to complete an activity that involves previously identified problems with decoding, such as vowel or consonant sounds, common prefixes and suffixes, digraphs, blends, or word families.

During-Reading Strategies

- As students read a selection, help them fill in the events in a story or the main facts in an informational piece in a visual organizer.
- Help students focus on key information by having them highlight or underline main ideas.
- Monitor off-task behaviors and help students re-focus: "Right! Where were we now? Oh yes, we were just getting ready to read about the part where Geoffrey is supposed to pick up the traffic cone. What do you think might happen?"
- Talk out loud about reading strategies you use while reading and encourage students to do the same.
- Model an effective reading strategy and give students lots of opportunities to practise it. For instance, you might read aloud, "Bina adjusted her chador and went outside." Then you might say, "I can't remember if the chador is the long garment that covers her whole body or just the scarf that covers her hair and shoulders. I'm going to look back, skimming for the word 'chador' to see if I can find out."

Strategies for Tutoring Students with Learning Disabilities (continued)

- Keep track of any decoding problems and create activities that provide practice in the problem. Be sure to show students the progress they are making over time. For example, the prefix *trans-* might have been causing the student a comprehension problem. The prefix would be noted in the tutoring plan and at the next session, the student would do an activity using *trans-* to create and define a number of words with this prefix, such as *transformation, transatlantic, transfer*. When the student more easily understands passages using words with the prefix *trans-*, show the date on which the problem was noted and praise the student for effort and progress.

- Use key rings or boxes with 3 X 5 file cards to help students keep a personal dictionary of previously taught words and definitions.

- Show students how to use context clues to determine the meaning of a new word or phrase.

- As they read a text, have students fill in a graphic organizer, either on paper or on the computer.

After-Reading Strategies

- Return to the graphic organizer or anticipation guide used earlier in the lesson and have students review the main events or ideas in the text.

- If you have access to a computer program such as *Kidspiration, Inspiration,* or *Smart Ideas,* ask students to map the main ideas or events from the text. Then, have them use the button that puts that mind map into a linear outline (the hierarchical feature) to write a short report or paragraph, moving back and forth between the graphic organizer and linear writing.

- Prompt students to write down the answers to previously prepared questions or questions that arose during the reading of a text. In textbooks, questions appear at the end of the section. In other instances, you might prepare a few questions.

- Review the accuracy of predictions made before the reading began.

- Have students complete a previously prepared reading guide to focus on specific issues such as comprehension, inference, vocabulary, and text structure. Such guides are typically prepared by teachers for completion by the whole class. If students are reading texts other than those being read in the class, you will need to prepare a guide. If this is the case, ask the classroom teacher for a few samples on which to base it.

- Review any reading problems related to decoding.
  - Ask students to identify the applicable rule and provide another demonstration of it. Example of a rule: *The letter "e" is usually silent when at the end of a word.*

- Tell students to write short personal responses to what has been read. Their reading log entries could be done by hand or with a computer and should always be dated.

Learning Disabilities: An Official Definition

One of the three major types of learners that reading tutors may be asked to work with are students with learning disabilities, which are defined fully below.

"Learning Disabilities" refer to a number of disorders which may affect the acquisition, organization, retention, understanding or use of verbal or nonverbal information. These disorders affect learning in individuals who otherwise demonstrate at least average abilities essential for thinking and/or reasoning. As such, learning disabilities are distinct from global intellectual deficiency.

Learning disabilities result from impairments in one or more processes related to perceiving, thinking, remembering or learning. These include, but are not limited to language processing; phonological processing; visual spatial processing; processing speed; memory and attention; and executive functions (e.g. planning and decision-making).

Learning disabilities range in severity and may interfere with the acquisition and use of one or more of the following:

- oral language (e.g. listening, speaking, understanding);
- reading (e.g. decoding, phonetic knowledge, word recognition, comprehension);
- written language (e.g. spelling and written expression); and
- mathematics (e.g. computation, problem solving).

Learning disabilities may also involve difficulties with organizational skills, social perception, social interaction and perspective taking.

Learning disabilities are lifelong. The way in which they are expressed may vary over an individual's lifetime, depending on the interaction between the demands of the environment and the individual's strengths and needs. Learning disabilities are suggested by unexpected academic under-achievement or achievement which is maintained only by unusually high levels of effort and support.

Learning disabilities are due to genetic and/or neurobiological factors or injury that alters brain functioning in a manner which affects one or more processes related to learning. These disorders are not due primarily to hearing and/or vision problems, socio-economic factors, cultural or linguistic differences, lack of motivation or ineffective teaching, although these factors may further complicate the challenges faced by individuals with learning disabilities. Learning disabilities may co-exist with various conditions including attentional, behavioural and emotional disorders, sensory impairments or other medical conditions.

For success, individuals with learning disabilities require early identification and timely specialized assessments and interventions involving home, school, community and workplace settings. The interventions need to be appropriate for each individual's learning disability subtype and, at a minimum, include the provision of

- specific skill instruction;
- accommodations;
- compensatory strategies; and
- self-advocacy skills.

The official LDAC definition of learning disabilites has been printed with permission from www.ldac.ca, the official Web site of the Learning Disabilities Association of Canada, Ottawa, Ontario. Phone: (613) 238-5721; Fax: (613) 235-5391; E-mail: information@ldac-taac.ca.

All About Me

Name: _____   Nickname (if I have one): _____

Age: _____   School: _____

Courses I am taking right now and teachers' names:

Course	Teacher

Foods I like to eat _____

TV shows I like to watch _____

Songs, groups, or kinds of music I like _____

Hobbies I have _____

Pets I have and their names: _____

Sports I like to watch _____

Sports I like to play _____

If I could have four people—dead or alive, real or fictional—to lunch with me, I would invite

_____   _____

_____   _____

If I was stranded on a deserted island and could have just one piece of reading material with me, it would be

_____

If I could change one thing about myself, it would be _____

One thing I would never change about myself is _____

Beyond that, one thing I'm good at is _____

I think a good friend should always _____

Student Profile Summary

Name: _____ Age: _____ Grade: _____

Strengths	
Interests	
Experiences	
Learning Style/ Multiple Intelligences	
Learning Needs	
Suggestions	

Reading Interest and Attitude Survey

Name: _____   Date: _____

Question	Student Response
What are some of your earliest memories about reading?	
Did your parents read to you? If they did, what are some stories you remember?	
What do you remember about how you learned to read?	
Did you have some favorite books when you were young? What do you remember about them?	
What makes reading a positive experience for you?	
What makes reading difficult for you?	
What kinds of reading material do you find the most interesting? the least interesting?	
Do you sometimes have difficulty pronouncing words? If so, what do you do when you come to a difficult word?	
Do you sometimes have difficulty understanding what you read? If so, what do you do when that happens?	
Have you ever worked with a tutor or someone who tried to help you before? What worked? What didn't?	
What kinds of texts do you prefer to read? Newspapers? Magazines? Graphic novels? Novels? Stories? On what subjects?	
What kinds of movies, television programs, and computer games do you like to watch or play?	
How can I help you with your reading? What would you like to work on?	

Tutoring Plan

Student: _____ Date: _____

Student Profile/Interest: _____

Lesson Topic	
Learning Outcomes/ Expectations	
Tutoring Session Goal	
Learning Materials	
Before-Reading Activities	
During-Reading Activities	
After-Reading Activities	
Strategies for Addressing Special Needs	
Observations/ Feedback/ Assessment	
Reflections	

Simple Diagnostic Reading Assessment

Student's Name: _____ Date: _____

Title of Reading Passage: _____

Make observations based on the following questions.

Decoding Questions: While reading, does the student

❑ Skip words?

_____

❑ Guess unknown words based only on the first letter or two?

_____

❑ Substitute words that make sense in the sentence?

_____

❑ Substitute words that do not make sense, but fit with sentence syntax (structure)?

_____

❑ Pause when reading aloud?   (never   sometimes   often)

_____

Comprehension Questions: During reading, does the student

❑ Notice when the words are not making sense?

_____

❑ Try a fix-up strategy? (Examples: slowing down, rereading, pausing and thinking)

_____

❑ Make predictions about what will happen next?

_____

❑ Ask questions and clarify ideas?

_____

❑ Read with appropriate expression and phrasing that communicates sentence meaning?

_____

❑ Pay attention to punctuation? (Examples: pausing at periods, having the voice go up at the end of questions)

_____

Ask a few questions when the student is done reading and make notes.

Comprehension Questions: After reading, can the student

❑ Retell the main idea?

_____

❑ Provide relevant supporting details to the main idea?

_____

❑ Make a personal connection to an idea in the text?

_____

❑ Describe a main character's actions (if the text is a narrative)?

_____

❑ Explain the problem and the solution (if the text is a narrative)?

_____

With the initial administration of this assessment, the teacher will normally provide information about items in the Comprehension sections, such as the main idea and relevant details.

Genre Inventory

Name: _____

Kinds of Books/Texts I Like to Read	A Lot	Somewhat	Not Much
1. Fiction			
a) fantasy	❏	❏	❏
b) horror	❏	❏	❏
c) science fiction	❏	❏	❏
d) adventure	❏	❏	❏
e) suspense	❏	❏	❏
f) mystery	❏	❏	❏
g) romance	❏	❏	❏
2. Non-Fiction			
a) biographies	❏	❏	❏
b) autobiographies	❏	❏	❏
c) textbooks	❏	❏	❏
d) newspapers	❏	❏	❏
e) magazines	❏	❏	❏
f) letters	❏	❏	❏
g) e-mails	❏	❏	❏
h) diaries/journals	❏	❏	❏
i) manuals	❏	❏	❏
j) interviews	❏	❏	❏
3. Poetry/Lyrics	❏	❏	❏
4. Drama	❏	❏	❏

Interest Inventory

Name: _____

Topics That Interest Me	A Lot	Somewhat	Not Much
Sports such as _____	❑	❑	❑
Animals such as _____	❑	❑	❑
Humor	❑	❑	❑
Relationships (family/friends)	❑	❑	❑
Fantasy	❑	❑	❑
Music	❑	❑	❑
Visual Art	❑	❑	❑
Drama	❑	❑	❑
Dancing	❑	❑	❑
Biography/Autobiography about _____	❑	❑	❑
Games	❑	❑	❑
Television Programs and Personalities	❑	❑	❑
Films	❑	❑	❑
Vehicles	❑	❑	❑
Nature/Outdoors	❑	❑	❑
The Environment	❑	❑	❑
Popular Culture	❑	❑	❑
Science	❑	❑	❑
History	❑	❑	❑
Romance	❑	❑	❑
Crafts/Hobbies _____	❑	❑	❑
Computers/Technology	❑	❑	❑
War	❑	❑	❑
Health	❑	❑	❑

Web Sites with Information on Choosing Books for Young Adults

- **http://guysread.com** The Web site of the Guys Read non-profit literacy initiative was founded by Jon Scieszka and is supported by him, the New York Foundation for the Arts, and Penguin. The site offers lists of books recommended by Guys Read users for guys of all ages, from young boys to adults.

- **http://www.ala.org/yalsa/booklists** The American Library Association's Young Adult Library Services Association lists current award-winning books, DVDs, videos, and audio books on its Web site.

- **http://www.sharyn.org/children.html** This site features many lists of literacy organizations with book recommendations for adolescents as well as children. There are also discussions of issues facing reading teachers. Among the organizations represented are the International Reading Association (U.S.); IBBY (the International Board on Books for Young People); the Children's Book Council; the Cooperative Children's Book Center (Univ. of Wisconsin); the Children's Book Council of Australia; the Canadian Children's Book Centre; the National Council of Teachers of English (U.S.), and its Assembly on Literature for Adolescents.

- **http://www.teenink.com/Books** Run by Teen Ink, The 21st Century and The Young Authors Foundation, Inc., this site offers book reviews written by teenagers and a place for teenagers to submit their own book reviews.

- **http://www.ipl.org/div/teen** This Internet Public Library site, sponsored by the University of Michigan, provides book reviews (including graphic novels) as well as information about a variety of Web sites of interest to teenagers, from clubs and organizations to homework help and sports, entertainment and the arts—all vetted by the University of Michigan.

- **http://www.kidsreads.com/index.asp** This site is part of the Book Report Network, founded in 1996 to provide information about books to kids. The site targets youth in the Grades 5 to 9 age range. Books are not identified by recommended reading level, which is a drawback. Although intended for youth to access reviews of books that might be of interest, the site is equally valuable to teachers and tutors for information on new releases.

- **http://www.teenreads.com** This site is also part of the Book Report Network. Here, teenage readers will find a rich mixture of book suggestions and information. Benefits and drawbacks are the same as for kidsreads.com.

- **http://teenlink.nypl.org/index.html** This New York Public Library site identifies recommended titles for young adults.

- **http://www.acs.ucalgary.ca/~dkbrown/index.html** On this University of Calgary site are suggestions about Canadian books for children and teens.

- **http://www.readingonline.org** The International Reading Association features its top book choices for teachers, children, and adolescent readers here. There are subject, title, and author indexes.

Probable Passage: Non-Fiction Model

Title of Selection: _____

Envelopes labelled with categories

Slips of paper with key words from text

Slips of paper placed into appropriate envelopes

Some Map and Chart Organizers

Story Map

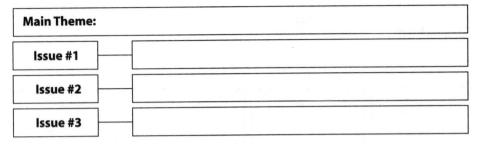

Main Theme:

Issue #1	

Issue #2	

Issue #3	

Main Characters

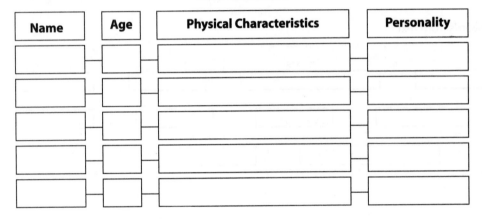

Name	Age	Physical Characteristics	Personality

Plot Map

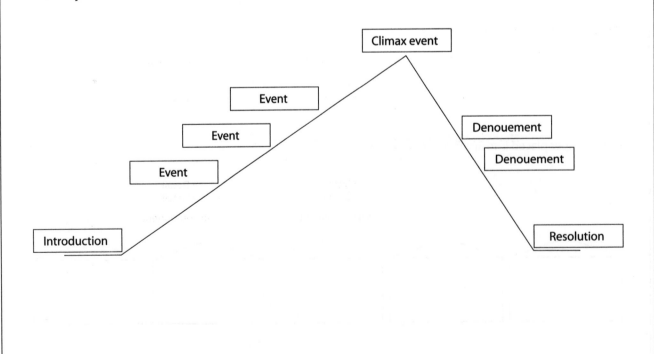

Climax event

Event

Event

Event

Introduction

Denouement

Denouement

Resolution

Some Map and Chart Organizers (continued)

News Story Map

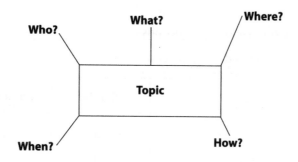

Sequence Map for an Essay

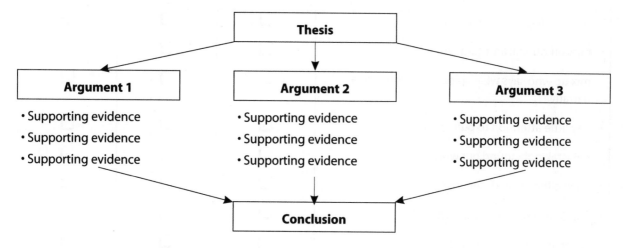

Fishbone (Herringbone) Chart

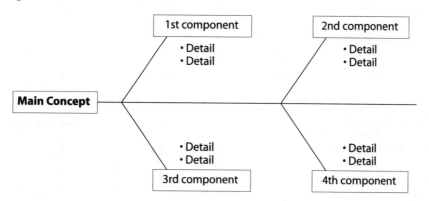

Fluency Checklist

Name: _____ Date: _____

Length of passage: _____

Silent reading time: _____ minutes and _____ seconds

Oral reading time: _____ minutes and _____ seconds

When reading aloud, does the student	Rarely	Sometimes	Often
• stop frequently?	❏	❏	❏
• make inappropriate pauses?	❏	❏	❏
• read word by word?	❏	❏	❏
• speak in flat, monotone voice?	❏	❏	❏
• miss emotional and contextual cues?	❏	❏	❏
• mix up who says which piece of dialogue in a narrative?	❏	❏	❏
• pay little attention to punctuation?	❏	❏	❏
• painstakingly sound out words?	❏	❏	❏
• have difficulty with sounds?	❏	❏	❏
• fail to recognize recurring words?	❏	❏	❏
• emphasize the wrong syllable?	❏	❏	❏
• ignore suffixes and prefixes?	❏	❏	❏
When reading silently, does the student			
• read at about the same speed as when reading aloud?	❏	❏	❏
• shift eyes often on the page?	❏	❏	❏
• need to stop and reread often?	❏	❏	❏
• seem to skim large chunks of text?	❏	❏	❏

Comments and next steps:

Books to Help Develop Fluency

Picture Books

Bosak, Susan V. *Dream: A Tale of Wonder, Wisdom and Wishes.*

Bridges, Ruby. *Through My Eyes.*

Browne, Anthony. *Voices in the Park.*

Burleigh, Robert. *Hoops.*

Poetry and Readers Theatre

Fleischman, Paul. *Joyful Noise: Poems for Two Voices.*

Fleischman, Paul. *Big Talk: Poems for Four Voices.*

Graves, Donald. *Baseball, Snakes and Summer Squash: Poems about Growing Up.*

Kennedy, Caroline, ed. *A Family of Poems: My Favorite Poetry for Children.*

Swados, Elizabeth. *Hey You! C'mere: A Poetry Slam.*

Young, Judy. *R Is for Rhyme: A Poetry Alphabet.* (also a picture book)

Note: See www.aaronshep.com/rt/index.html for Readers Theatre script books.

Books

Datlow, Ellen, and Terri Windling, eds. *A Wolf at the Door and Other Retold Fairy Tales.*

DiSpezio, Michael. *Awesome Experiments in Force and Motion.*

Jocelyn, Marthe, ed. *Secrets: Stories Selected.*

Bibliography

Adams, Marilyn. 1996. *Beginning to Read: Thinking and learning about print.* Cambridge, MA: MIT Press.

Anderson, R., E. Heibert, J. Scott, and I. Wilkinson. 1985. *Becoming a Nation of Readers: The report of the Commission on Reading.* Champaign-Urbana, IL: Center for the Study of Reading.

Beattie, J. 1994. "Characteristics of Students with Learning Disabilities and How Teachers Can Help." In *Teaching High Risk Learners: A unified perspective,* edited by K. D. Wood and B. Algozzine. Toronto: Allyn and Bacon.

Beer, Kylene. 2003. *When Kids Can't Read: What teachers can do, A guide for teachers 6–12.* Portsmouth, NH: Heinemann.

Bennett, B., and C. Rolheiser. 2001. *Beyond Monet: The artful science of instructional integration.* Toronto: Bookation.

Berrill, D. P. 2006. *Building Literacy Skills through Tutoring and Computer Assisted Intervention.* Report for the Literacy and Numeracy Secretariat, Ontario Ministry of Education.

Blanton, L. P. 1994. "Providing Reading Instruction to Mildly Disabled Students." In *Teaching Reading to High Risk Learners: A unified perspective,* edited by K. W. Wood and B. Algozzine. Toronto: Allyn and Bacon.

Booth, David. 1998. *Guiding the Reading Process.* Markham, ON: Pembroke Publishers.

Bos, C. S., and S. Vaughan. 1988. *Strategies for Teaching Students with Learning and Behavior Problems.* Boston: Allyn and Bacon.

Clark, K. 2004. "What Can I Say Besides 'Sound It Out'? Coaching word recognition in beginning reading." *The Reading Teacher* 57(5): 440–49.

Clay, Marie. 1993. *Reading Recovery: A guidebook for teachers in training.* Auckland, NZ: Heinemann.

Collins-Block, C. 1997. *Literacy Difficulties: Diagnosis and instruction.* Toronto: Harcourt Brace College Publishers.

Cooter, R. B., and D. R. Reutzal. 1994. "Instructional Techniques for Making Subject Area Material More Comprehensible for Readers at Risk." In *Teaching Reading to High Risk Learners: A unified perspective.* Boston: Allyn and Bacon.

Fisher, D., and N. Frey. 2004. *Improving Adolescent Literacy: Strategies at work.* Upper Saddle River, NH: Pearson.

Fisher, D., et al. 2004. "Interactive Read Aloud: Is there a common set of implementation practices?" *The Reading Teacher* 58(1): 8–17.

Gardner, H. 1993. *Frames of Mind: The theory of multiple intelligences.* New York: Basic Books.

Green, J., and M. Winters. 2006. *Leaving Boys Behind: Public high school graduation rates.* Civic Report No. 48. New York: Manhattan Institute. Available online at www.manhattan-institute.org.

Griffith, L., and T. Rasinski. 2004. "A Focus on Fluency: How one teacher incorporated fluency with her reading curriculum." *The Reading Teacher* 58(2): 126–37.

International Reading Association. 2004. *On Reading*. A position statement. Newark, DE: IRA. Available online at www.reading.org.

International Reading Association. 2000. *Making a Difference Means Making It Different: Honoring children's rights to excellent reading instruction*. A position statement. Newark, DE: IRA. Available online at www.reading.org.

Murray, S. 2006. *Re-assessing Literacy: Challenges for Canada*. Edudata Forum: Vancouver, May 5, 2006.

NCTE. 2004. *On Reading, Learning to Read, and Effective Reading Instruction: An overview of what we know and how we know it.* Urbana, IL: NCTE (National Council of Teachers of English). Available online at www.ncte.org.

Ogle, Donna. 1986. "K-W-L: A teaching model that develops active reading of expository text." *The Reading Teacher* 39: 564–70.

Ontario Ministry of Education. 2002. *Reaching Higher: Supporting Student Achievement in Literacy*. Toronto: Ontario Ministry of Education. Available online at www.edu.gov.on.ca.

Ontario Ministry of Education. 2003. *Think Literacy Success: The report of the expert panel on students at risk in Ontario*. Toronto: Ontario Ministry of Education.

O'Shea, L. J., and D. J. O'Shea. 1994. "What Research in Special Education Says to Reading Teachers." In *Teaching High Risk Learners: A unified perspective*, edited by K. W. Wood and B. Algozzine. Toronto: Allyn and Bacon.

Stauffer, P. G. 1975. *Directing the Reading–Thinking Process*. New York: Harper & Rowe.

Sternberg, R. J. 1985. *Beyond IQ: A triarchic theory of human intelligence*. New York: Cambridge University Press.

Tovani, C. 2000. *I Read It, But I Don't Get It: Comprehension strategies for adolescent readers*. Portland, ME: Stenhouse Publishers.

UNESCO. 2003. United Nations Decade for Literacy. See www.unesco.org.

Wasik, B. A., and R. E. Slavin. 1993. "Preventing Early Reading Failure with One-to-One Tutoring: A review of five programs." *Reading Research Quarterly* 28(3): 179–200.

Weber, Ken, and Sheila Bennett. 2004. *Special Education in Ontario Schools*, 5th Edition. Palgrave, ON: Highland Press.

Wolf, M. 2003. *What Is Fluency?* Research Paper, Volume 1. New York: Scholastic.

Wood, K. 1984. "Probable Passages: A writing strategy." *The Reading Teacher* 37: 496–99.

Wood, K. D., and B. Algozzine, eds. 1994. *Teaching Reading to High Risk Learners: A unified perspective*. Boston: Allyn and Bacon.

Ysseldyke, J. E., and S. L. Christensen. 1987. "Evaluating Students' Instructional Environments." *Remedial and Special Education*, 8(3): 17–24.

Index